LOVED
ON A
GRANDER
SCALE

LOVED ON A GRANDER SCALE

AFFIRMATION, ACCEPTANCE, AND HOPE
FOR WOMEN WHO STRUGGLE WITH THEIR WEIGHT

Neva Coyle

VINE
BOOKS

SERVANT PUBLICATIONS
ANN ARBOR, MICHIGAN

Unless otherwise indicated all Scripture quotations are from the Holy Bible, New International Version, copyright 1973, 1978, 1984 by International Bible Society. Used by permission of Zondervan Publishing House. All rights reserved.

Scriptures indicated KJV are from the King James Version of the Bible. Scripture verses marked NASB are from the New American Standard Version of the Bible. All rights reserved.

Although the stories in this book are true, names and identifying characteristics have been changed to protect the privacy of the individuals involved.

Vine Books is an imprint of Servant Publications especially designed to serve evangelical Christians.

Published by Servant Publications
P.O. Box 8617
Ann Arbor, Michigan 48107

98 99 00 01 10 9 8 7 6 5 4 3 2 1

Printed in the United States of America
ISBN 1-56955-066-2

LIBRARY OF CONGRESS CATALOGING-IN-PUBLICATION DATA

Coyle, Neva, 1943-
    Loved on a grander scale: affirmation, acceptance, and hope for women who struggle with their weight / Neva Coyle.
        p.   cm.
    Includes bibliographical references.
    ISBN 1-56955-066-2 (alk paper)
    1. Weight loss—Psychological aspects.   2. Weight loss—Religious aspects—Christianity.   3. Christian women—Religious life.   4. Body image in women.   5. Self-esteem in women.   I. Title.
RM222.2.C664   1998
155.6'33—dc21
                                                          98-22588
                                                          CIP

CONTENTS

INTRODUCTION

"You're not really going to write this book, are you?" The voice of my longtime friend and respected coworker rang with disbelief.

"I have to," I responded with conviction. "I have never felt more called or qualified to address a topic as I have this one."

Do you know what it's like to have your life, worth, and purpose sharply defined simply because you are a certain size? I do. In fact, I can't imagine anyone knowing what that's like better than I do.

You see, I have been thin. And with thinness came all kinds of accolades and publicity. *Free to Be Thin* was written in 1979, and within a very short time more than a million copies had been sold worldwide. My writing career was formed and shaped—not around my talent but around my size. Ministry was launched—not based on my calling or my ministry gifts but because of the size of my body. Everybody wanted to hear what I had to say—not so much because I had something worth saying but because I had lost weight.

Then one day that all changed. I regained the weight. Painfully and even publicly, I got fat again.

Yes, once again, I have had to square off with the fear of fat, face to face. And so have many of you. I know this because hundreds of people have written to me not only about their own fear of fat but because of my own painful weight regain. So many wrote, in fact, that I found it necessary to produce a little brochure with my entire story written concisely and in a way that I hoped would help others understand what was happening not only to me, but also to them!

My Story

In 1984, when *Free to Be Thin* was selling nearly ten thousand copies a month and my speaking schedule was in high gear, I was stopped dead in my tracks by a severe health crisis. By spring of 1985 I could no longer delay the inevitable; not only was my health in jeopardy but also my life. At the advice of my doctor and the counsel of the Overeaters Victorious board of directors as well as my family and my pastor, I tearfully surrendered to surgery to reverse an intestinal bypass I had undergone sometime before.

During the year that followed, I gained sixty pounds. With each passing year, it was increasingly difficult to keep my weight in check. My doctors predicted that I would probably regain all the weight I had ever lost, and I was even warned that I might end up weighing more than ever, all while maintaining responsible, healthy eating habits. But, they assured me, something good would come out of it: I would live, and in all probability I would be healthy once again.

Can you imagine my emotional reactions, thoughts, and perceptions of what was happening to me? Can you also imagine the many varied but understandable reactions that were sure to come from my readers? These were the people —the ones I loved and ministered to—who caused me to make the difficult decision to have the surgery. If you have ever lost and regained weight, you have an idea of the inner struggle and personal turmoil I faced.

Even now, more than ten years later, it still causes me personal pain to see the reaction of some people as they hear about my weight struggle for the first time. However, faced with the choice of giving up or going on (though at times it would have been far easier to give up), I chose to go on. I chose to embrace the idea of God's love and a continuing plan for my life regardless of my size. It wasn't easy.

I was forced to take another look at weight issues. Before long I began to wonder what it would actually take to live at peace with my body as a large person. Was there support for such a wild idea—getting off the weight-loss bandwagon once and for all? Could I find the courage to live normally as a large person? Would others accept my decision? And more importantly, would they eventually accept me as something other than an unfortunate, misguided quitter?

I began my search in a medical-school library and quickly discovered much information concerning stubborn weight, including solid, scientific information about the challenges of maintaining significant weight loss. These journals supported what I already knew to be true from my own painful experience. In the past I had never been open to reading, much less to applying to my own body and life, the facts contained in these medical journals. I read these journals and was amazed that I hadn't seen what should have been readily evident all along. And once I started digging I was more than amazed. I was angry.

Angry that I had been so unmerciful and shallow with myself and other large Christians. Angry that no one had guided me differently when I made decisions that risked my life and health in order to be slender. Angry that it had taken me so long and had cost me so much to finally realize that one reasonable alternative to weight management was healthy management of my large body. Angry that I had never before considered that one perfectly legitimate solution to my weight struggle was to focus not on the weight but on ending the *struggle*.

Adjusting My Attitude, Not My Dress Size

With caution and much prayer, I began to consider that God might be bringing me full circle concerning weight issues and personal worth. Did this understanding and acceptance come easy? Absolutely not. Never have I waged a war so intense and personal as the one I fought to finally accept myself and my large body. No spiritual warfare has ever been as powerful and unrelenting as was the battle to step into my full worth as a valued member of God's family as a large woman.

The struggle was tremendous, but the final result has been worth the fight. The Lord has given me the freedom to be myself and to accept my size. He has also given me a deeper understanding and a more insightful sensitivity to overweight people than ever before. In the past, I looked at all overweight people, myself included, as undisciplined overeaters who simply needed to surrender this area to Christ. People who, through prayer and discipline, could expect the fat to easily melt away. However, I now understand that is not always the simple truth.

You see, I now know that not all overweight people are overeaters, and not all overeaters are overweight. In other words, I have learned that lifestyle does not always connect in such an uncomplicated way with size. I have long since repented of this simplistic and self-righteous position. With new understanding I am now more able than ever to minister to people who are disillusioned with weight-loss promises, struggling with painful weight regain, or finding that they are getting heavier each year without really changing their eating habits or lifestyle.

Some people have suggested that I have given up. But I haven't.

Some believe a book like this is simply my way of justifying my weight gain. But that's not true.

Yet I must admit I have given up demanding that my life go exactly as I plan. I have given it up to God. Under His control I surrender completely to His purpose and plan for my life. As a result, hope still burns brightly within me—with one major change: My hope can no longer be extinguished by the bathroom scale. No matter what I weigh, I trust in God and have accepted His enduring, unchangeable love for me.

I am ready to be as honest and open as I can be about my own struggles as well as my victories. It is sometimes tempting to look back at the years of pouring my life into ministry, teaching, retreats, seminars, and writing and in the light of one critical remark about my size, toss it all aside, and curl up safely within the loving and protective arms of my family and church. However, without a doubt, I know God has more planned for me than that.

The Pain of Regain

Do *you* know what it's like to have your life change simply because you are a certain size? If you have lost weight, you are the champion, the victor, the star. But if you've put on a few pounds, you're the loser, the beaten, the overlooked. Isn't that what we've been told and have told ourselves over and over again?

Yet in westernized culture the fear of fat is justified. Not because of the fat itself but because the social and emotional consequences of regaining weight are absolutely horrible. So why not just go off and lose it again? Then what? Again and again? Going through this repeatedly throughout the remaining years of my life isn't an option for me any longer. I've more to do with my life and energy than to give in to the whims of my body or the culture that defines it and my worth based on its size.

But this acceptance of myself as a large woman is much harder than I expected. Of course, being the author of the *Free to Be Thin* Christian weight-management material didn't help matters at all. Surely you can imagine the double takes I receive when I appear at a book-signing or step up to the podium for a speaking engagement. Weight regain is painful enough when handled within one's social and family circles. But when it's the business of the entire Christian community and Christian publishing industry, it's downright scary!

Nevertheless, considering the pain of my weight-regain experience, I determined that God would not have allowed this situation in my life had He not had further use for my life and ministry beyond what I knew before. So with His help, I dug in. I read. I searched "the Net." I bought books. I scanned the Scripture. And little by little, I found the courage to face, up close and personal, the fear of fat. And once I got beyond the tears, I learned several interesting facts.

Out of the Fat Race

There are literally thousands of women who have had it with the insanity of trying to fit into a culturally prescribed ideal that is impossible for about 95 percent of all adult females.

A once-successful model wrote, "It has taken me many years to forgive myself for not maintaining the rigid 125- to 130-pound model mandate—and to forgive the fashion industry for requiring mannequins to be paper-thin."[1] Boy! Do I understand that statement.

For most of my adult life, I've carried the stigma of being large. I've heard all the remarks, and if you're overweight, so have you. For years I labored to be thin, to fit in. All I wanted was to be average. In the United States average is a size 14, but when I got there, I wanted to be a size 12, then a 10. Endangering my health and jeopardizing my life in the process seemed a reasonable risk to me. After all, I hated being fat, hated the way I looked, and for one entire horrible day, even considered death preferable to ever being fat again.

However, there's been a change in all that. I have embraced what God's Word says about me. Although I'm a "woman of size," God's Word includes me as a person of value, someone who has worth. The plan of salvation is not reserved for the thinnest, most envied 5 percent of the population. It's for every person—large, small, short, or tall. **An intimate relationship with God isn't size dependent. Even at my largest, God loves me. And no matter what you may believe at this moment, He loves you too.**

I don't care how your present body is shaped or what it looks like. No matter if you are scarred from traumas, surgeries, or stretch marks, your body is fearfully and wonderfully made. It matters not if you are disfigured, puffy-cheeked, or freckled, Jesus Christ shed His precious blood that you might have the opportunity to live in intimate relationship with God, our Father. You have no reason to feel wasted and unlovely one moment longer. You are a cherished child of God.

Now, I can't explain the mysteries of the gene pool. I don't understand why my sister is thin and I'm not. Even though we were both raised in the very same environment, she can eat far more food without the same physical consequence of weight gain. Why is that? And why is it that our thin sisters can eat more without feeling as if they have committed a crime? It's unfair, but for many of us it's a fact of life.

I know how it feels to be categorized and stereotyped on the basis of appearance alone. But I have learned that God never does that to me. One of the purposes of this book is to help you experience the same love and acceptance from our loving Heavenly Father.

You Are Not Alone

Your feelings of being a social outcast or of being ugly or never quite good enough may not come from being larger than culturally acceptable, but the resolution is the same. Perhaps you have been made to feel that you're the wrong color or are less than pretty or have a misshaped chin. No matter what has robbed you of the joy of recognizing yourself as a magnificent creation of God, it's time that all came to an end.

I think it's time to take the necessary steps toward God's unconditional love and let Him do a deep work within us to restore our souls. Maybe we never will measure up to society's standard or even the church's image of acceptable physical appearance, but I'm convinced we can get beyond it. As Christians we can have a sense of value and purpose as we place our hope in Christ—and Christ alone.

As you read this book, remember that my negative experience has been mostly with my weight. But I have also experienced the less-than-acceptable status of being from a low-income, single-parent family. I know what it feels like to never quite measure up, to never belong to the "in" crowd. But being fat is like no other challenge. For many it is the primary source of painful struggles related to appearance and self-acceptance. I want to change that. As you read this book, I ask you to look deep within the heart of its message for the hope you deserve and long for.

After twenty years of ministry in what is now being called the Christian weight-control movement, I realize that a person's weight issues are far more complex than we once thought. I have even come to believe that while we are all destined to be free in Christ, not all of us were meant to be thin. Size variability is a fact of life. Being a woman of size is not a sin, and our bodies are not our enemies. It's time we recognize that our *biology* has more influence on our body size than our *theology* does.

So, have I really joined the Fat Power groups? Have I wholeheartedly accepted the entire philosophy of the Size-Acceptance Movement? Not at all. I'm not a militant shouting for rights. Furthermore, this book is not a cry for sympathy or help, and it's *definitely* not an attempt to justify my size or validate my painful experience.

I'm simply a Christian who thinks it's time to come back to the basic belief that *whosoever* will may come to Christ and find acceptance and individual worth. That close encounters with a living God are open to all equally. That all of us can experience the freedom Jesus bought for us at Calvary.

Through God's Word and a close love-relationship with Him, we can walk in victorious release from the tyranny of weight, appearance, and image obsessions. I want to proclaim to everyone who will listen—large, slim, beautiful, or plain—that there is freedom from food obsessions, and there is liberty from stereotypical bondages and boundaries. I want to announce to hurting, misjudged people of both the secular and Christian world that while man may look on the outer shell, God never does so. Jesus Christ knows and loves the real, inner me.

My hope is that I can reach other large people like myself who are hurting. Whether you are twenty-six or sixty-six years old, it is time you stopped letting your worth be defined and your life be ruined by rude stereotypes that demean people of size or unkind attitudes that criticize those considered less than perfect.

It's time someone stood up and said it: *I'm loved! Loved on a grander scale!* And it's time you knew His love too.

Now, don't expect this to be a book about taking license and liberties with this newly found freedom. I'm still a very strong proponent of personal responsibility and accountability toward God in all areas of our lives—including food and personal health habits. I don't intend to bash and blame the church or toss the personal-responsibility factor out the window. However, I am no longer afraid to look at prejudicial views about fat women and men. I will no longer run away from saying something quite new. The message on the following pages is one of freedom, liberty, and hope. It's filled with love and mercy, understanding and tenderness toward you and your personal-worth struggles. You deserve to know that you are loved. Loved beyond anything you have ever known before. More than you could even imagine.

At the end of each chapter, you will find a prayer. I hope you will let it be your prayer or let it be a model for your own personalized talk with God. Let's begin with this one:

*F*ather in heaven, I confess to You that I have listened to prejudicial comments about my body and have taken on guilt for how You made and designed me. I confess my sin of being ungrateful for my body; I have hated the way it looks and works. I have even accused You of being unfair with me for the way I look. Liberate me, I pray, from the pressures to be anything other than what You want me to be, both physically and spiritually. Help me, Lord, to embrace Your love, to accept the fact that You love me on a much grander scale. Amen.

Section One

WHY DO I HAVE TO BE THIN?

Chapter One

WHERE DOES IT ALL BEGIN?

"Do you have any nonfat ice cream?" Kylie asked the counter attendant.

"Nonfat?" Kylie's mother interrupted. "Are you on a diet?"

"Yeah," Kylie explained. "My butt's too big."

"Who told you that?"

"Kenny Mason. He says I'm as big as a whale."

Sounds like a teenager's comment, right? Guess again. Kylie is six years old. Kenny is five. Both are already prejudiced by our cultural ideal of skinny. Kenny knew exactly how to insult Kylie and ruin her birthday party.

Is it really that bad? Yes, I'm afraid it is. Even at the age of five, some American females fear being fat more than anything else—even more than dying or being painfully crippled.

Little girls are praised for looking pretty, and their little brothers are praised for their performance. And it doesn't get better with time; it gets worse! I've heard it again and again since being sensitized in the area of appearance obsessions. Sometimes those fate-filled words come out of my *own* mouth.

One Sunday night at church, a young girl barely eleven years old sang a lovely, well-rehearsed number. "Such a petite little thing," an older gentleman observed. Not one person commented on her courage to stand on the platform alone. No one mentioned the memorization and practice it took to deliver the rendition so well. Nor did I overhear anyone mention her selection for its fine message. Even though those things took place, most comments were along the lines of "What a tiny thing she is, standing up there all alone," or, "Why, she's no bigger than a minute." The one I cringed at the most was, "What a grown-up little dress you have on. Is that new?"

Every comment referred to how she looked. Not one word commended her for how hard she had worked or what a great talent she had shown. No one assured her that the Lord had ministered through her song. No one said God had blessed her with awesome talent for His kingdom and glory.

But it isn't only in our church families that such tragic mistakes are made. What about the emphasis on child beauty pageants? Would you be surprised to know that one four-year-old's parents routinely spend $350 on a hair-and-makeup stylist and upwards of $500 or more on a dress for a single competition? How's such a young child supposed to react when her mother dissolves in tears when she comes in only second?[1]

Yet the most damage is done right in many homes. "Daddy's little princess," her father says adoringly to his little girl while telling her little brother, "You are getting so smart, young man."

A father's remarks about his wife's hips, waist, or bust, whether disparaging or complimentary, also make a lifelong impact on a young girl. So do the cutting comments he makes when a large woman walks in front of the car. By the time she is four or five years old, "Daddy's little girl" knows what Daddy likes and doesn't like about a woman's body. If fat is on the top of his no-no list, Princess determines she'll never be fat—never!

Couple Daddy's remarks with Mommy's latest diet craze or exercise fancy, and Princess knows that whatever you are in life, you can't be fat. By the age of six, Princess has probably either been on a diet (of her own choosing) or thinks she should be. All it takes is a "Kenny" remark, and she knows for certain she's fat. It's the one thing in the world she fears more than anything else.

The simple fact is this: Kids caught up in image obsession are younger than ever before.[2] When a six-year-old hates the way she looks in a bathing suit because her bones don't stick out like her skinny friend's do, there's something wrong.

Stuck in Barbieland

Immersed in the appearance-perfect media while being influenced by their parents' obsession with health and nutrition reports and exercise programs, how can girls help it? Deceived by the illusion that thin and pretty equal happiness and success, many little girls dress their Barbie dolls and swear, "I'll look just like this when I grow up." Anything less would be failure.

Is it any wonder many of our ten-year-old daughters and granddaughters are attending sleep-overs where the discussion centers on who's fat and who isn't? Do we question why these precious children point out their own perceived body flaws and exchange ideas on how to thin down their thighs and build up their breasts? Are we surprised they prefer an ab-roller to the jungle gym? A Cardio-Glide over a seesaw?

All too soon, they turn on each other. "Many girls," says Dr. Mary Phipher, "become good haters of those who do not conform sufficiently to our culture's ideas about femininity. Like any recent converts to an ideology, girls are at risk of becoming the biggest enforcers and proselytizers for the culture. Girls punish other girls for failing to achieve the same impossible goals that they are failing to achieve."[3]

"At thirteen," Dr. Phipher continues, "many girls spend more time in front of a mirror than they do on their studies. Small flaws become obsessions. Bad hair can ruin a day. A broken fingernail can feel tragic.

"Just at the point when their bodies are becoming rounder, girls are told that thin is beautiful, even imperative. Girls hate the required gym classes, in which other girls talk about their fat thighs and stomachs. One girl told me of showering next to an eighty-five-pound dancer who was on a radical diet. For the first time, the girl said, she looked at her body and was displeased. One talked about wishing she could cut off the roll of fat around her waist. Another thought her behind was 'hideous.'"[4]

And right at the age when they are becoming adults rather than just children, we are abandoning them, encouraging them to seek a perfect rather than a real self. Think about it. Wasn't there a day in your life, as there was in mine, when you decided your body wasn't your friend but the enemy after all?

For me, that day didn't come at the age of six or seven or even ten. It came at the age of fourteen when my aunt took me shopping for a new dress. "My goodness," said my four-foot-eleven, size-6 aunt. "You *are* a big girl, aren't you?"

I was already five feet, six inches tall and wore a size 14. She announced I would not be wearing a full-skirted dress to my cousin's wedding. "Let's not bring any more attention to your hips, OK?"

I was devastated. I didn't know my hips were all that big. As soon as she left the dressing room I turned to view my backside in the mirror. I didn't appear to be any different than before. So I redefined what I saw. I was *fat!* Right then and there I decided it must be so. If my aunt said I was, I was. How could I have not known this before?

"It's probably just baby fat," my aunt said once we were in the car and headed toward home. "If you're careful, you'll be all right. It might even go away by itself."

If I'm careful? It might *go away? What if it doesn't? I'm not all right. I'm fat!* The entire family would know before dark; I was sure of that. I wondered what my mother would say when she learned I was fat. Did she know? Why hadn't she told me this before?

I went to the wedding, and I wore the straight-skirted dress. But, conscious that I might be offensive with my big hips, I kept my sweater on and my backside safely against a wall the entire time. I was, after all, different now. Not more grown-up. Not smarter. But fat. *How awful!*

Without any help from my personal doctor, without even

weighing myself, I decided I was fat based on my much-loved aunt's opinion of what would be better for me. I felt like an Amazon next to my diminutive auntie. After all, she was older, so she must be right. I assumed that my parents hadn't told me for their own reasons, which I guessed ranged from loving me too much and not wanting to hurt my feelings to the possibility that they really didn't care about me at all. Typical adolescent mood swings kept me from asking.

Unlike girls today who discuss their body flaws and exchange advice on how to get rid of them, I kept the awful secret to myself. Eventually I entered high school and learned to pay more attention to my hair and makeup. *Draw attention to your face, away from your hips,* I decided. I piled on layers of stylish petticoats in a futile attempt to hide my forbidden hips, but never, ever wore the straight-skirted dress again. And the straight skirts with sweater sets other girls wore? Forget it. No, I cinched a belt around my waist until I could barely breathe. I scrunched my oversized self and multilayered skirts into schoolroom desks as the tourniquet-tight belt cut into my middle. The discomfort convinced me that I was more than fat! I was as big as a cow! Too fat, too ugly—worth nothing.

Of course I knew about diet pills, diet candies, and other diet aids. My aunt was taking them, her daughter was taking them, and by this time my mother and older sister were taking them too. But I didn't try that until much later, after I was married.

Today it's different. Today, any teen is fat. At least that's what almost every one of them would say if asked. Popular literature on this subject estimates that 70 to 90 percent of teenage girls suffer from a negative body image! Sadly, the younger the teen, the higher the percentage.

Today, if a young woman decided to confide her fat fears to someone, she would most likely seek out the advice of a thin friend who had fat fears all her own. "Oh, my gosh!" the skin-and-bones friend would probably say. "I know just how you feel. Look at *my* thunder thighs, would you? What are we going to do?" From peer pressure to peer counsel. Out of the frying pan into the fire.

Can fads and fallacies do anything except flourish in such fertile young minds when fueled by fear and prejudice? If these precious young girls don't feel like they fit into the pretty and picture-perfect set, they can find plenty of friends in the "ugly-as-sin" set. And the cycle begins. Is it any wonder a twenty-three-year-old newlywed diets her way through her first pregnancy? And her young husband will probably support her in worrying as much about her weight gain as the baby's! After all, he's been raised in the same fat-intolerant atmosphere as his wife.

But before we get into husbands and beauty issues, try to think back to when you were first made aware that you were less than acceptable. Was it because you were fat that you decided you were less than OK? Or was it just because you *decided* you were fat? How much did you weigh then? Would you like to weigh that much now? Looks quite different from here, doesn't it?

I was only fourteen. I didn't even know what I could or would become at that age. Until that day I had even enjoyed cartoons and paper dolls. I loved to be with my mom and cook and sew. I loved to ride my bike and look at the sunset, watching for the first star to appear in the desert sky. School was exciting, and reading was like exploring an entirely new world with each new book. At that age, boyfriends were not much more than fancy, wishful thinking. But that day, that fateful day, I learned I was fat, and everything changed. Life lost its fun. I had one pressing responsibility, one mission in life—to get thin. I took the challenge as if it were a divine calling.

Someday, when my Prince Charming arrived to carry me off to get married, I would be a beautiful, *thin* bride—I took the oath. I decided to become somebody else—a *thin* somebody else. And secretly, with no adult supervision or advice, I went on my first diet.

How about you? When did you discover this same "shameful and shocking" fact of life? When did you take up the challenge to become somebody else? When did you take the oath?

$\mathcal{D}$ear God, help me to see that I no longer need to be bound by the immature and uninformed decisions I made so long ago. Help me to see how much You loved me then and how much You love me now. I've rejected my body because it didn't fit my definition of perfect, because according to my own opinion, I didn't measure up as ideal. I have believed the lie that my body somehow represents my worth. I have been angry at You because You made me this way. I confess that I have not trusted You in this area. To know You love me just the way I am hasn't helped before this. Please, dear Lord, I want to be what You want me to be. To be all You want me to be. Help me to be just that and nothing more, nothing less. Please, dear Father, set me free to be me. Amen.

Chapter Two

BEING THIN FOR HIM

f My Fair Lady were written today, it would not be a story about changing Eliza Doolittle's speech, clothing, or manners but rather about changing her face and body. Using methods from face-lifts to miracle diets to liposuction, women in increasing numbers are striving—with a degree of panic and, more often than not, to their own detriment—to match the ultimate template of beauty.[1]

But women aren't the only ones who have been affected severely by our national obsession with weight and our glorification of thinness and appearance. So have our men—our fathers, brothers, and most of all, our husbands. It's not so much that this attitude impacts our husbands' own body images (although that is rapidly changing) but their image of their wives' bodies. Many married women not only live with their own unachievable physical standards but are emotionally doubled over trying to live up to their husbands' expectations.

If a wife is an approval junkie, the load is unbearable. Abbie is a good example.

Abbie always gets up an hour before her husband, Mike, so that she can have the bathroom to herself while she gets ready for work. She never allows Mike to see her without her makeup and hairstyle intact. As she slips out of bed, she hastily tugs her nightgown down, just in case her husband awakes. If he should see those extra five pounds around her waist, there would be trouble. Mike insists that Abbie be a perfect size 6.

On the other hand, I know a wonderful, charming woman who weighs nearly three times what Abbie weighs. Andrea (not her real name) dresses in colorful styles that flatter her beautiful skin and frame her lovely face. Eric, her husband, frequently takes her hand as they walk together on the beach or at the mall. He slips his arm protectively around her shoulders at church and, even after twenty-five years of marriage, enjoys taking her on dream vacations. She is, by all current definitions, fat. He isn't.

What makes the difference between husbands such as Eric and Mike? Why is Andrea free to be herself and dearly loved while nearly body-perfect Abbie isn't?

Is the problem with the husbands? Could the answer lie within the wife? The answer to each question is yes, no, not really, perhaps, and more. Confused? Let's take a look at our culture for more insight. What I call the Barbie-and-Ken mentality. It has victimized us all.

Keeping Yourself Only Unto Thin ...

There is a certain charm to having a darling wife. It boosts a man's ego, makes him look good in the eyes of other men. In a fiercely competitive world, a darling wife gives other men reason for envy. Or so a man thinks. If he can't measure up out in the open world and marketplace, behind closed doors he's in heaven. At least he wants other men to think so.

Let's be truly honest. How many of us have ever been impressed, either positively or negatively, by the wife of the CEO where we work? Think about that Christmas party when she came out looking either like a glamour queen, or like the plain, motherly type. Didn't your opinion of *him* undergo a moment of adjustment when you saw *her*? How about the wife of a popular Christian TV personality, a famous preacher, or even your pastor? We prefer "done" but not "overdone." Stylish but not too bold a fashion statement, of course. But *fat?* Never! It just wouldn't do. Thin is much better; tiny is even better yet. Am I right? You know I am.

A fat wife is rarely seen as an asset; more often, based on her body size alone, she's seen as a liability. In our thin-worshiping culture, the professional man or common laborer is affected by the size of his wife. It's not fair—not to him, not to her. But it's true.

Overconcern with what people think of us, our mate, and our body is accompanied by a fear of rejection—of not measuring up. And when that fear takes hold, we create lives based on decisions made strictly to guarantee approval and acceptance.

This addiction to approval often dictates what we wear, what we say, and how we behave. It also leads us to try death-defying feats to keep our bodies within socially acceptable boundaries and size limits.

It's as if some invisible dictator is demanding conformity to an unattainable ideal. It overwhelms us with the need to be physically perfect if we are to amount to anything at all. And sadly, our husbands are under the same perfection pressure we are. The difference? They don't feel pressured to be thin themselves; that burden is placed squarely on the shoulders of their wives.

Unfortunately, as some husbands begin to yield to this pressure, they begin to regard their wives' bodies as personal property to be shaped, molded, curtailed, and expanded at will.[2]

Geri can attest to that situation. Her husband, Mitch, insisted that with breast augmentation Geri's body would be perfect—that he'd be satisfied at last. Geri followed her mother-in-law's suggestion and consulted a plastic surgeon. "Body contouring," he explained, "is simple, safe, and most satisfying."

On the day of her scheduled transformation, she paused. "Do I really want to do this?" she asked herself out loud. "Is this really the right thing for me to do?"

"For me," Mitch urged. "Do it for me."

So Geri did it. She slipped into unconsciousness, and the surgeon sliced the fold beneath each breast and inserted a silicone implant. Mitch was elated.

Seven months later, Geri's immune system let her down. Catching colds frequently was only the beginning. Soon she became the victim of every virus going around. Her breasts were becoming firm, too firm, and finally they became hard and rigid as scar tissue grew around the leaking implants.

A pain-filled year later, Geri was alone. Packing her Christmas decorations away the day after Christmas, she prepared for the surgery to follow. Spending the holiday without Mitch had been bad enough, but facing a double mastectomy without him was nearly unbearable. Mitch? He'd opted for another, larger-chested woman. Will Geri have reconstructive surgery? "Not right now," she said tearfully. "Maybe never. I just want to be well again."

Thankfully, not all husbands go to such lengths or cause such damage to their wives as Mitch did. Many resort to much more subtle sabotage with unkind remarks about their wives' hips, thighs, or torso. Sometimes these remarks are made on the heels of an admiring comment about someone else's hips, thighs, or torso. Since a wife has only one body to offer her husband, the rejection can be overwhelming. And since she can't separate from her body, the rejection hits hard and deep.

I'd like to say that the husbands who put such intense pressure on their wives to be perfect are *not* Christians. The truth, however, is that many are. In fact, there are many more of them than we can possibly imagine. Letters like this one from Imogene tell the tragedy.

"I don't know what to do," she wrote. "My husband says if I don't lose weight he'll leave me. That I'm driving him to adultery and that his sin will be on my head."

I shook my head and kept reading. "I've gained with each baby. No matter what, I can't take off those last few pounds. My husband calls me *Gordo*. Can you help me? I'm only five-foot-six and almost up to 150 pounds! He says I'm disgusting to him and a disappointment to God. I've given up singing in the choir at church and also teaching Sunday school. I'm such a poor witness for Christ."

A poor witness? At 150 pounds? Perhaps you are as shocked as I was. Many reading this book would love to weigh 150 pounds. Many more would like to get their hands on Imogene's husband. But wait. Let's look at how many of our husbands, even Christian husbands, are influenced by the media of our day.

Each and every day our homes are invaded with messages of perfection that are seen as normal, even average. Starting the day with Lisa McRee or Katie Couric doesn't make me look any better before nine A.M.—how about you? Through movies, magazines, and TV, we see beautiful people as often as we see our own family members. The net effect is to make exceptional beauty appear real and attainable. The modern woman has television, in which she doesn't see herself reflected.[3] Studies of prime-time television indicate that programs are dominated by thin body types and that thinness is consistently associated with the portrayal of favorable personality traits.[4]

It makes us feel that many of our own features are flawed, even those having to do with weight or appearance. We are stuck here in a world of obsessive self-criticism, where what we see is not at all what we really are.[5]

Our husbands are also inundated with perfect images by the same programming we watch. They pick up the same subtle false messages—physical perfection is achievable.

Writing for *Psychology Today*, Judith Rodin said, "The vast majority of American women have accepted at face value the message we have been continually exposed to: that beauty and physical perfection are merely a matter of personal effort and that failure to attain those goals is the result of not doing enough."[6]

Wow! If I believe that, I'm in big trouble. If my husband believes it, our *relationship* is headed for trouble.

Unless a husband decides to unburden himself from the

lies of unattainable perfection, thinness, and beauty, his overweight wife will always carry the knowledge that she is a disappointment to him. As a result the woman of his dreams can come to feel like she is his worst nightmare. It can crush the life right out of her. When a husband heaps criticism and disapproval because of appearance or body size on his wife who is already struggling with her own sense of worth and value, the damage may be irreversible—to her, to him, and, tragically, to them as a couple.

It's not only the media that influence our husbands. Many men, even Christian men, come with emotional baggage left over from childhood. Issues of control may be at the core of many complaints about our bodies. If we then turn to food to dull the pain of unhappy feelings caused when our husbands complain about our appearance, and if we gain weight when we overeat, making them complain all the more ... can you see the problem? As self-defeating as it is, overeating sometimes results from a power struggle, not only with hubby but also with parents, siblings, or even ourselves.[7]

Criticism never, ever helps when we're already burdened by an obsession with thinness and beauty. Any unasked-for comment can be viewed and defined as hostile disapproval. Sarcasm and ridicule wound deeply, and it doesn't help to have a husband deny any malicious intent with comments such as, "I'm only kidding—can't you take a joke?" or, "You're too sensitive. Can't you tell when I'm teasing?"[8] Once the harsh words are spoken, it's too late to undo the damage; the blood is already dripping from a fresh emotional wound.

Someone has to ask: How much of ourselves do we have to give up to be loved by the men to whom we have pledged our lives? Someone also needs to ask our husbands how much they are willing to give up so that we can be ourselves at last.

A Suitable Helper?

Both Christian husbands and wives caught up in the American (or perhaps westernized) image obsessions have to return to God's Word for help. We were never meant to be assets but helpmeets. *Suitable*, Genesis 2:20 says, not perfect. *Helper,* not trinket.

How much did Eve weigh, anyway? How would the very first woman on earth fare in our beauty-pageant mentality? How would the Proverbs 31 woman compare to the *Baywatch* babes of today?

"Charm is deceptive," says Proverbs 31:30, "and beauty is fleeting." When will we get that through our self-oriented and media-saturated minds? When will we give rewards that have been *earned* and bestow praise for good *works* rather than good looks? (see Prv 31:31).

When will we be seen as persons instead of bodies? When will we stop being defined by our appearance and our weight?

Will it stop when our husbands stop defining us by those things? Maybe not. Maybe it's as much our responsibility as theirs. Perhaps our husbands will see us as real persons when we choose to be ourselves. Maybe they'll stop trying to be *Kens* when we stop being *Barbies*.

Can we actually help our husbands become more sensitive toward us and our weight and worth struggles? Maybe not. But when we choose to let God love us just the way we are, when we decide to be what God intended us to be, when we finally allow ourselves to find our value in eternal issues rather than external appearance, there's bound to be a change in the way we're treated by others. Even by our husbands.

*D*ear Lord, help me to see how I can view myself as a real person, valued and precious apart from my husband's opinion, value, or attempts to control me through my appearance or weight. Give me the strength to duck his criticism or cruel remarks—even when he's only teasing. Set me free, Father, free to be me—just like You made me to be. Then give me a heart of forgiveness toward unkind remarks and selfish efforts to control me, strengthen me with a new love for my husband, and give him a new, freer love for the new free me. Amen.

Chapter Three

AT WHAT PRICE BEAUTY?

"*I*t's gaudy, it's fake, it's real, it's live! We hate it. We love it!"[1] It's Atlantic City, it's Regis and Kathie Lee—it's Miss America time. And one young woman will be crowned out of over fifty thousand contestants. Her gossamer dream will come true. Her year as the epitome of American beauty and perfection will begin. Since the beginning of the pageant in 1921, almost every young girl has wanted to be Miss America. Not just to be beautiful, not just to be noticed, but to be judged and then crowned more beautiful than all the others.

While the dream of being Miss America is far from the reality of a young girl whose life is filled with acne and bad-hair days, the obsession with weight, beauty, and appearance isn't. Feeling like the high school loser, perceiving herself as fat and misshapen, life can become almost unbearable for a teen in the image-obsessed American culture. "I just want to fit in," the adolescent moans. "I'm as fat as a pig!" Large, average, small, or even skinny, many girls sing the same song. "My nose is too big! My ears stick out. I'm ugly!" they cry as they tuck the latest issue of *Seventeen* magazine into their backpacks.

Does this sound too immature or worldly to apply to mature, spiritually healthy women like us? We probably couldn't manage to enter, much less win the pageants, but we have our own competition just the same. We may not pay the entry fees and buy the gowns, but we still enter the perfection competition. You see, we no longer want to look *our* best. We want to look *the* best. *The very best!* And we often do whatever we can for as long as we can to attain the look we long for.

While it may not be as emphasized elsewhere as it is in California, concern about one's physical appearance and fitness is now a nationwide preoccupation. Widely seen by many as vain, the vanity and fitness cult, which is Californian in style and roots, shows no signs of abating. In fact, it's spreading. What's worse, it's an obsession we applaud, an addiction to which we willingly give ourselves over. And what's worse, we've welcomed it into the church.

In our culture the ability to fit in to the very narrow ideal of physical perfection is seen as power. The goal is not just to look good but to look perfect.[2] In church circles, we may not recognize the perfection goal as a play for power, but have we defined it as inner strength of character and spiritual maturity?

In the late 1970s many of us were motivated toward self-improvement. Healthy enhancement. Fitness and improved self-control. But something happened to us along the way, and we got hooked. We became driven to look like Barbies and Kens.

But there are no real-life Barbies, no real-life Kens. In fact, to measure up to the ideal of the Ken doll, the average man would have to be seven feet, six inches tall, boast a twenty-four-inch neck, a fifty-three-inch chest, and a forty-four-inch waist. And the American woman? To match the original

Barbie doll, she'd tower above the rest of us at eight feet, six inches, flaunt a forty-five-inch bust, and a twenty-six-inch waist.[3]

"But I don't want to be perfect," you may protest. "I just want to be better!"

All well and good. But given the obsession with the distorted concept of *perfect*, do we even know what *better* is? Better than what? Than whom?

As much as we hate to admit it, we've become not only victims but perpetrators of an unwritten code of beauty. We build our own beauty identities with the makeup, hair, and skin-care rituals acceptable in our little collectives bound by friendship and age where we live, play, and work. Even at church we stick to certain appearance rules. And although there are no national standards, no massive do's or don'ts, we act like there are—or at least in our circles, in our clubs, cliques, and churches. Whether we wear the makeup look of the sixties with our hair back-combed and shaped into bee-hives and our eyes lined in liquid blue or go for the totally "natural" look of taupe eye shadow and heather-colored eye pencil outlining our lips, we are bound by a beauty code. And sometimes that beauty code is so strong it controls the entire life of the appearance-obsessed person.

"We depend so much on externals to judge people— makeup, hair, clothing, weight," explains family therapist and author Christine Brautigam Evans. "We watch for people to stay within certain bounds. It sounds shallow, but we are assessment machines."[4]

The Model Image

Even in the church, much of what we think we ought to look like comes from the pages of our magazines and from our TV screens. Beautiful models sell everything from adhesives to the state of being "Zest-fully clean." Even though they don't speak or even move, these images are seen more frequently and feel more familiar to avid readers of magazines than their own relatives and distant friends do.

But the reality is that we're looking at a false person. The person in the picture is a fabrication, an image projected by the stylist or the photographer. I don't know about yours, but my bathroom mirror doesn't feature the subtle effects of a misty lens, backlighting, or attendants fussing with my hair and makeup. It's just me and my generic self standing there in the early morning. *That* image is reality-based, whether I like it or not. To survive such an experience, it is in my best interest to have my value and worth based in something *other* than how I look.

I once heard a story about a newspaper columnist who was watching a group of long-legged blondes at a Hollywood party. "If you look like that," she moaned, "you're interchangeable. But if you don't, you're invisible."

Perhaps you and I don't have that same pessimistic view of life (or even of blondes for that matter) but do we feel invisible? Do we feel as though we've been divided into two groups—the acceptable and the unacceptable? And what would happen if we were caught without our hair done and makeup on? Would we be forced to change groups?

"Oh, come on," you might be saying. "It's not that bad."

No?

Did you know that over seven million American women suffer from eating disorders? Are you aware that a recent study revealed that 60 percent of sixth-grade girls said they had dieted to lose weight? Body image is a major concern not only in our nation but in our towns and in our churches. Can you name one teenage girl that you know personally who is completely satisfied with her body? Or, like the contemporary norm, can most teenagers you know tell you down to the littlest detail what is wrong with theirs?

It's not uncommon for young women today to spend a high percentage of their waking moments in front of a mirror, searching their reflections, studying what they perceive to be abnormalities with a magnifying glass. While the most severe cases of what is called body dismorphic disorder are chemical in nature, it is frightening to even think about where our obsession with beauty and flawlessness is leading our young women. Full-blown BDD patients in need of professional care aren't the only ones in a constant and exaggerated state of worry over their appearance.

How about you? Have you ever stayed home simply because you couldn't decide what to wear or because you were having a bad-hair day? Or been so preoccupied with the thought that the jeans you decided to wear accentuated your hips that you spent the entire day backing away from people? Have you ever been distracted during a church service because you were convinced that the dress you had on made you look dumpy or fatter than usual?

The Surgically Re-Imaged

A woman wrote that her friends had advised her to stop complaining about how she was aging and get out and consult a plastic surgeon about her "slipping forehead." After all, she reported, "I am your average thirty-seven-year-old woman who, between the ages of thirty-two and now, seems to have aged overnight."[5] And she's not alone.

Surveys reveal that up to 95 percent of all women have a flabby body image. Body images are often so distorted because no matter how many laps we swim, no matter how much iron we pump, we'll still never measure up to those perfectly chiseled, airbrushed beauties who prance around the pages of sports-magazine swimsuit issues.[6]

But beauty-obsessed American women won't be defeated by age. No sir! Not when we can go to a surgeon who skillfully knows how to smooth out our wrinkles, lengthen, shorten, narrow, or widen our noses, stuff our flat breasts, or vacuum out unsightly mounds of fat from our thighs, tummies, or chins.

But a Christian woman wouldn't do such a thing, would she? No. Absolutely not. Of course not. After all, we're born again, cherished, beloved children of God. We're washed in the blood of Jesus, claimed as God's own. Named before the foundation of the world was even laid. Called out of darkness to share in His wonderful light. In Him we live, move, and have our very being. The Master, the Lord and Ruler of the universe, loved us even when we were steeped in sin and sorrowfully away from His wonderful plan for our lives. As saved women, wonderfully delivered from the power of

Satan and sin, we find our joy and delight in belonging to the Lamb of God. Our eyes are on things above, not on things of the world. We know this world and our existence in it is fleeting. We're bound for heaven to live forever. We're aliens and strangers in this life. Our destinies aren't in the superficial but in harmony with the supernatural. We are walking miracles, testimonies of God's grace, and firsthand witnesses of His mercy.

We are the bride of Christ. We would never, ever get caught up in such shallow practices and image-based obsessions. Right?

Wrong!

Thin ... for Him!

Our churches are filled with women who wonder how any man, much less God, would be interested in them unless they stayed pencil-thin, applied their makeup with the skill of a professional, and had every hair in place. We weave our tresses, blush our cheeks, and pierce our ears just like all the other women do. We cream and moisturize, we shave and pluck. We frost and highlight. We diet and even starve ourselves into oblivion.

And why?

Because we have bought the world's way of thinking ourselves acceptable based on appearance. On style. As if pleasing our heavenly Father depended on some westernized version of beauty.

Now, before you throw this book across the room or toss

it into the wastebasket, let me clarify something. I'm not advocating that plain is any better than fancy when it comes to appearance. All you'd have to do is look at my French manicure and my "berri-pretti pink" toenails to know that I'm not suggesting that we go back to the stark, barefaced look of legalistic piety.

But I do think we need to take another look here. Not because of our appearance, but because of our *obsession* with our appearance.

I've always been curious about the passage of Scripture found in James 1:23-25.

> Anyone who listens to the word but does not do what it says is like a man who looks at his face in a mirror and, after looking at himself, goes away and immediately forgets what he looks like. But the man who looks intently into the perfect law that gives freedom, and continues to do this, not forgetting what he has heard, but doing it—he will be blessed in what he does.

It's a familiar passage to most Christians, because it has to do with looking into God's Word and letting it change us. It's what we have come to know and quote often when we say, "Be doers of the Word, not just hearers only." But I see something more. Something buried within this familiar text is almost a curiosity, in light of our current beauty and appearance obsessions.

Look at these words: "... a man who looks at his face in a mirror and, after looking at himself, goes away and immediately forgets what he looks like."

Wow! Can somebody do that? Is it possible to forget what we look like? Even for one moment?

There is no way in the world we can stretch and bend this biblical comment into a command. The Bible is not saying here that we must look in the mirror and immediately forget what we look like. No. Rather, the biblical writer simply chose that illustration as a normal thing to do. He used something that was known to illustrate a concept less known. He compared a normal thing to looking into God's Word and going about your day forgetting what God's Word said.

In our day, that illustration or example wouldn't work as well. For we are most conscious of how we look almost every minute.

Think about it. Our bathrooms and bedrooms are lined with mirrored walls. A mirror hangs in the dining room or over the living-room couch. Perhaps a small mirror hangs by the front door. Leaving our homes and heading for work each morning, we take our mirrors with us. Lighted "vanity" mirrors grace our sun visors. Even in public buildings we are favored with well-lighted restrooms and, you guessed it, mirrored walls. Department stores, grocery stores, you name it. Reflections of our images are everywhere. And sitting at a table in a restaurant? Just reach into your purse. Surely you have a mirror in there someplace, right? It would be pretty difficult to forget what we look like, wouldn't it?

And yet, I'm not even referring to the availability of mirrors as a problem. I'm referring to those who, because of an appearance obsession, *must* have them available. Those who simply cannot live without having them at hand every minute.

Relieved that I'm not talking to you? Good. But you see, this chapter had to be included because there are those who can't live any meaningful existence at all apart from their appearance. I'm serious. Obsessed with how they look, they must reassure themselves every moment that the image they worked so hard to create in the morning is still there at mid-morning, at noon, at midafternoon, and so on. Their own image is the center of their world. And, sad but true, I'm convinced there are Christians who live like this each and every day of their lives—simply because they have accepted without question the world's message. The message that says as long as they look good, they are good. That if the outside is right, the inside is right.

Are we so westernized, so indoctrinated by our appearance-obsessed culture, that we are deceiving ourselves? I believe it to be true. And what's more, I believe many Christians are convinced that we can look like the world, talk like the world, and act like the world and yet not be affected by the world. Such deception puts us in grave danger.

We're in danger because when our obsessions are anything other than loving and worshiping our living Lord and Savior Jesus Christ, we have taken our eyes off of Him. When we buy into the world's system of acceptance based on appearance, we no longer operate by God's system of being made acceptable by the shed blood of His only Son, Jesus.

Please don't get me wrong. I'm not promoting ugliness

as holiness. I love my perfume and pretty hairdo as much as anybody. But obsessed? That's where we must draw a line. *Balance* is the key word. In my opinion, balance is what 1 Peter 3:3-4 is all about.

> Your beauty should not come from outward adornment, such as braided hair and the wearing of gold jewelry and fine clothes. Instead, it should be that of your inner self, the unfading beauty of a gentle and quiet spirit, which is of great worth in God's sight.

When we pay close attention to this passage, we see that it doesn't say we can't wear nice hairstyles, gold jewelry, or lovely clothes. Just that our real beauty does not come from those things. Our beauty comes from letting God free us on the inside, deep inside us where our *real* identity lives. It comes from letting God work deep within our hearts and souls to heal us, make us new, eradicate the scars left by life, and give us not a face-lift but a heart-lift! This kind of beauty will never fade. It's a quiet, deep *inner* beauty that radiates from our eyes, perhaps eyes accentuated with subtle shades of pearlescent shadows—or not. It's beautiful words that come from the quiet heart, even through lips that are covered with creamy-rose lipsticks—or maybe not. It's lovely, healing touches given by hands that are soft and manicured—or maybe not so soft and pretty. It's open faces bearing expressions of hope and trustworthiness—perhaps touched and enhanced with foundation and just the right amount of blush, or perhaps not.

The point is this: If the beauty of Jesus is seen in me, it no longer matters that I find it impossible to look like a photographer's model. You see, I'm not here to represent me anyway. I'm here to live for and represent Him. Freed from the obsession to be like or look like the world's unachievable image of beauty, I am now free to be me—just me—just the way He made me to be.

Thank You, Heavenly Father, that You created me to be unique and that my individuality is important to You. I'm grateful that Your requirements all rest on Jesus Christ and not on my being or doing or looking some certain way. Thank You that I belong to You and that You never criticize me for the way I look or how much I weigh. Help me, Lord, to please You in my heart and life. Help me serve You in the unique way You planned for me, and give me strength to live among those who may think less of me because of my appearance. Thank You for loving me on a much grander scale than the world uses to measure me. Amen.

Section Two

WHAT HAVE I DONE TO MYSELF?

Chapter Four

BEAUTIFUL IS NOT
THE SAME AS LOVABLE

*W*hen a large person, especially a woman, decides to live life to the fullest in our thin-obsessed culture, one of the first obstacles she has to overcome is the overall sense of being somehow "unacceptable." Fat stereotypes are forever presenting themselves, and common myths about being large hit us squarely in the face almost daily.

Too Fat to Work: Size Discrimination on the Job

Discrimination based on body size alone is alive and well in the marketplace. About 40 percent of women who responded to one survey indicated that they had suffered from weight discrimination. They found themselves on the outside when it came to work-related social events and received negative comments from supervisors. Discrimination was doled out by degrees, they reported. The heavier the woman, the worse and more blatant the acts of discrimination became.[1]

Kate was fired after six months on the job because she simply "didn't fit in." Her work? Impeccable. Her offense?

"I can't prove it," she explains, "but I suspect my size 34 had everything to do with my termination."[2]

Whether you are a flight attendant or a sales representative, your size can adversely affect your chances in the job market.[3] Meeting the fear of fat face to face means we have to face it and deal with it creatively, positively.

Socially Svelte—or Silently Struggling?

Coming to terms with the fear of being fat doesn't improve your standing with the social set either.

Leslie Lampert found that out by donning a "fat" suit and braving her way into a fat-biased society. On her first venture out as a "fat" woman she wrote, "I take the commuter train to work. No one sits next to me. I feel incredibly self-conscious. People look long enough to let me know they disapprove, then go back to reading their morning newspapers. Two women go so far as to whisper blatantly, glaring at me with a how-could-you-let-yourself-get-like-that attitude. I take up one and a half seats, and yes, I feel embarrassed. Yet shame takes a backseat to the resentment I'm feeling. How dare these people judge me on the basis of my dress size?"[4]

Welcome to my world, Leslie.

And at church? Maybe a bit better than in secular society, but not by much. More polite, perhaps, but better? The signals are still there—thin is still in.

It's not easy facing people every day who sincerely believe that if you wanted to badly enough, you could lose the weight and keep it off indefinitely. Even I cowrote a best-selling book that promised "how to get thin and stay thin forever." But I now know the truth: Permanent weight loss eludes most fat people. Most of my sources in my research from the early eighties until now have concluded that the success rate is rarely above 5 percent! That's right. **Between 95 and 98 percent of all diets fail the dieter over three to five years.** When you realize that this is a statistical fact, not a personal failure and not a character flaw, it introduces you to the fear of fat head-on.

I understand Deborah Gregory when she says, "It's sad but true that most of us determine our ideal size by the a-woman-can-never-be-too-thin mantra that has seized our society. And, if we are in the dreaded category—a large woman—we are constantly on a diet or, at the very least, profoundly ashamed of our size."[5]

When I decided to meet my fear of fat face to face, it meant I had to look within for my own stereotypical attitudes toward large people, and that opened up even more mythological thinking that I harbored even against myself.

Myth #1: Thinner Is Always Healthier

While sedentary lifestyles do contribute to declining health and fitness levels, I could find no supporting evidence to indicate that a large person who was physically active and nutritionally conscientious should expect to be less healthy than a thin person who was also physically active and nutritionally conscientious. Most health sources agree that whatever your body size, it's far healthier to be either fat or thin than to yo-yo between the two.

I know this has certainly been true in my case. My own weight-reducing efforts put me on the path that eventually brought me near death. The sad fact is that I was healthier *before* I began my mission to be thin than I was when I became thin!

Myth #2: All Fat People Are Compulsive Overeaters

One challenging aspect of fighting the fear of fat is learning how to protect yourself from unfair assumptions made by others, particularly in the health-care industry. My friend Judy recently had an experience that illustrates this point.

It had been a tough year for Judy. For six months she had cared for her husband during his battle with lung cancer, herniating two disks in the process. Soon after her husband died, Judy left her job and moved to another city to be near friends. Then her diabetes raged out of control, and she made an appointment with a new doctor. Without asking any questions or even waiting for her medical records, he assumed that Judy's eating was out of control.

Judy had experienced plenty of pain and adjustment that year, but nothing had attacked her credibility as a person of worth and strength like that doctor's prejudicial attitude toward her weight. Fortunately, her background in the medical field gave her the courage to ask for a referral to a specialist. Once under the competent care of a specialist, her blood-sugar levels returned to normal, her food cravings abated, and she was well on her way to controlling her diabetes once again. She's now looking for a different primary-care physician.

Another lady told this story: "With my first pregnancy

my weight ballooned from 150 to 220 pounds, and I could never get it back down. I went to a doctor to get checked for a thyroid condition, but after the tests came back negative he said, 'Next time you go to McDonald's, don't order two Big Macs, large fries, and a shake. Order one Big Mac, small fries, and a diet soda.' That made me furious because I don't even eat at McDonald's. I wanted help, not condescension. I can get that from the whole world."[6]

Is it any wonder fat people rarely seek preventative medical care? Do doctors really question why large people put off seeking treatment when they do have a medical problem? Does anyone really doubt why overweight people hesitate to join a gym or take up power walking along public streets?

Meeting the fear of fat, face to face, meant that I had to learn to let people think what they wanted to think—without allowing it to affect how I felt about myself. Perhaps some thought I was a compulsive overeater. I'm sure there are those who think I'm lazy, undisciplined, and dishonest about how I feel about myself. Yet, I had to let it go. I knew better than anyone else how much food I actually ate.

Myth #3: All Compulsive Overeaters Are Overweight

Compulsive overeaters, whether fat or thin, are people with eating disorders. It is not true that every fat person you meet has an eating disorder. Studies have concluded that as a group, fat people do not eat more than thin people.[7] Individually, there are, of course, exceptions—in both groups, fat and thin. Compulsive dieters, on the other hand, are more likely to become obsessed with food and go on eating binges following a very low-calorie diet.

One writer quoted a woman who said, "The worst part about being overweight is that you wind up rejecting yourself because society rejects you. It's almost as if they're saying, 'If you can't control how much you eat, how can you control anything else in your life?'" says Michelle. "And you wind up putting blinders on because after a while it's hard to deal with all the negative attitudes."[8]

Myth #4: Fat People Are Ugly

I am an attractive woman. I have the same face, the same blue eyes, the same smile now as when I was thin. I keep my makeup and hairstyle nice. I dress in beautiful colors that complement my complexion.

However, since my weight regain I have had to stare down the myth that all fat people are ugly. People's ideas of beauty are learned, and they vary greatly from time to time and culture to culture. Lillian Russell, considered one of the most beautiful women of her day, weighed more than two hundred pounds. Even Marilyn Monroe would be considered "overweight" by today's standards.

The correlation between weight and beauty swings like a pendulum in our culture. Unfortunately, it will probably not swing back in my favor in my lifetime. But as Christians we can focus on an important truth: While worldly standards of beauty may change, our true beauty and value are measured by the loving eyes of our Heavenly Father. And God's Word encourages me with verses like this one from Deuteronomy 32:10-11.

In a desert land he found him, in a barren and howling waste. He shielded him and cared for him; he guarded him as the apple of his eye, like an eagle that stirs up its nest and hovers over its young, that spreads its wings to catch them and carries them on its pinions.

Myth #5: No One Will Love Me if I'm Fat

There is this really ugly misconception that large people cannot find anyone who will want to marry them. Not true. It is true, however, that those who would marry for more than "just a pretty face" (or as one Christian single put it, "a Barbie with a Bible tucked under her arm") still face the same prejudicial culture as the large women they may love.

While it is hard to be a large woman, even a large Christian woman, it may be just as difficult to be in love with one or be married to one. Why? Because the Bible says married we become as one. What hurts one spouse also hurts the other. Life is hard enough, some may reason; why make it any harder?

If you, too, have struggled with feelings of being unloved or unlovable, I encourage you to let go of these self-defeating thoughts. Recognize that your husband, no matter how loving and supportive, cannot build you up if you continually tear yourself down. On the other hand, nothing is more attractive to a man … any man … than a woman who is comfortable and confident in who she is.

Lessons of Life on a Grander Scale

If we are ever going to find peace with our bodies, we must first stop hating them. That means making friends with ourselves. Understanding that our bodies are where we live, not who we are.

It means that somehow we have to come to terms with lives that have been spent in fretting endlessly over food scales. We have to take a look at the shelf space taken up with calorie counters and diet books, not only in our homes, but in our hearts as well. Are we willing to abandon this obsessive preoccupation that threatens to overburden our lives until we die?

Making peace with our large bodies means we stop finding our value, or the apparent lack of it, in our size. We have to stop despising ourselves because of our weight. It's time we reclaimed the hope that we can actually be seen for ourselves—large, to be sure, but real and honestly ourselves.

So, What Has Changed?

I remember being thin. I remember the accolades that came with thinness. Not for my spiritual gifts of teaching, insight, wisdom, writing, and music but for being thin. I recall being seen as spiritually more in control simply because of my body size—an issue not really addressed in the Bible at all.

How could that happen? In our culture, a fat woman is seen as out of control, and a thin woman is perceived as being in control. And while both of those could be true in some cases, they certainly are not true in all cases. I had out-of-control days when I was thin, and I've had wonderful days of self-control since I've regained. I can't say I've had more self-control at either end of the bathroom scale.

I fight daily the feeling that somehow I should be dieting. That it's expected of me. That self-control isn't the real issue, dieting is. Should I live under an inescapable load of guilt that I'm not completely absorbed in my diet and preoccupied with the numbers on the scale? Have I really become distracted from what is essentially important to God because I've decided not to be emotionally consumed by my body size or appearance? Have I "lost the vision," as some critics have suggested? Shall I return to having the scale, rather than a close relationship with Jesus Christ, determine how I spend my days, my weeks, my life? Shall I really find my value and the purpose for my life in being thin rather than simply in trusting God's Word and will?

No, I have changed all that. I no longer see my body size as an *act* against God. I see it as a *fact* of life. Nothing more, nothing less. I can't please Him any less by being large or any more by being thin. I no longer feel condemned for getting hungry and eating a meal. And I've come to realize that stating my weight is not a confession of sin; it is what I weigh. I've allowed myself to once again feel satisfied with who and what I am. With the person God made me to be. With how He has gifted me and called me to ministry.

One day I stopped weighing myself and started appreciating where I've been and how much I've been through. I consciously chose to stop fighting against myself and embrace the life God has given me and the years I have left. Have I stopped hating myself for not being able to maintain a thin body no matter how much I try? I'm working on it.

I'm also learning to forgive myself for the years of abuse and self-criticism I heaped on my weary soul as I watched in horror as the pounds crept back. I'm pursuing release from the tyranny of an image-obsessed existence and have begun living a much fuller life in both body and soul. I've knelt at the foot of the cross and found that the love of Jesus covers me, even as a large woman. That He died for my sins just as He did for everyone else's. I've once again let Him reassure me that my life goes beyond this world's experience and prejudice. That nothing will be perfect until we get to heaven. And that as hard as it may be, as long as I live in rich, deep relationship with Him, nothing this old world throws at me will deter me from seeking His purpose and living His will to the fullest.

Yes, I have met the fear of fat face to face and stared it down. Was it easy? No. It's been the most incredibly difficult thing I've ever done. Did I ever back away? Oh, yes. Is it over? Probably not. But if you know me at all, the one thing you know is that I'm not a quitter. I will face this ugly fear again and again until it is gone. All gone.

The powerful encouragement of 1 John 4:18 shows me the way when it says, "There is no fear in love. But perfect love drives out fear." Would I rather be thin? Of course. But I am no longer willing to give my life and soul to it. I have better things to do. I have a family and am active in my church. I have wonderful friends and a speaking ministry that keeps my calendar full.

I'm an overcomer; I've known it for most of my fifty-plus years. If it wasn't this battle, it would be something else. I'm ready to move on. How about you?

I remember trying to think of something I'd rather be doing if I weren't so obsessed with my weight or appearance. I asked myself the question: If your image wasn't so all-important to you, what wonderful thing would take its place? Know what I answered?

Living!

Living completely and without inhibition—living for Christ. Using my gifts and energies for the kingdom and developing my spiritual muscles for kingdom purposes and spiritual warfare. I decided then to stop obsessing on my size and start living. Was it easy? Nope. Has it been worth it? More than I can possibly say.

*D*ear Jesus, forgive me for putting my body size before You. For spending so much time on how I look, how much I weigh, and caring more about pleasing others than I cared about pleasing You. Help me in Your perfect love to face the fear of fat and then walk in this new freedom, Your Majesty, to serve You no matter what my size and whether or not the world says I'm acceptable. I choose to live in Your love, for You and You alone. Amen.

Chapter Five

DIETING:
THE SURE WAY TO DEFEAT

*Y*ou might be thinking that since I have accepted my larger-than-average body as normal for me I have also changed my views on eating and perhaps dropped dieting practices altogether. If you are, you are right. I have made tremendous changes in my approach to food and even to life.

It's hard getting past what I know is expected of me. To boldly go where I thought I'd never ever go. But does that mean I have readopted old, careless eating habits and overindulgences? Not on your life.

I have simply accepted what I call a nondiet approach to food and nutrition. I don't count calories anymore. I don't beat myself up over a cookie or a piece of cake at a wedding. You see, the nondiet approach is *not* an uncontrolled lifestyle. I still have a heart to consider and good health to maintain. I'm still responsible for what I put in my mouth and how it affects my general well-being.

But diet? For me, it's a thing of the past. I agree with Joel Gurin, who wrote, "The old view of weight control was simple. People get fat because they eat too much, and they eat too much because they have a psychological problem with food. *[Only we said it was a spiritual problem, remember?]*

They overeat when they're depressed, excited, anxious, distracted or simply bored. If they could only learn new eating habits—take smaller portions, eat more slowly, stop their mindless munching—they'd lose weight. It's a neat, straightforward concept with just one flaw. It isn't true."[1]

If eating was the single underlying problem at the root of our size, all dieters would eventually be a size 0. Food in itself isn't the problem. Are we courageous enough to admit that? If I can't control my weight with a strict diet, do you suppose there is even a slight chance it wasn't meant to be controlled? Or could it be that food control might not be the same as weight control? Could there be cause for obesity other than excessive food consumption? If so, doesn't it merit another look, another approach altogether?

Now, don't get me wrong. I'm not saying it's OK if our *eating habits and food intake* are totally uncontrolled. I'm not advocating that we all become gluttons and give in to our every food whim and craving. Not at all! But if size weren't an issue, would food be? That's the question I came to grips with, and it wasn't easy. For me, the two had been so intricately locked together I had difficulty *seeing* them apart—much less *treating* eating and weight as separate issues.

So, what would happen if I decided on a nondiet approach? Would I even know how to begin?

No, I didn't, but I was willing to learn. So I began, with a promise from God's Word firmly secured in both mind and heart.

The Lord will fulfill his purpose for me; your love, O Lord, endures forever—do not abandon the works of your hands.

PSALM 138:8

Prayerfully, carefully, I took the risk. With God's help I gave myself permission to stop dieting. Then, with His help, I started all over again. I decided to learn how to eat. This may sound simple, but it wasn't. I was a professional dieter. I knew no other way to live. It was as scary as standing on the high-dive above the swimming pool when I was in the sixth grade. As I prepared to plunge into this new way of living I did again what I had done then. I held my nose and jumped.

No More No-No's

I took a good look at food. I changed my definition and stopped calling *any* food sinful. Bad and good were terms that no longer applied to food. Food was food. No more, no less. I realized that I could do harmful things to my body with it but that food in itself wasn't harmful. I gave myself permission to be normal. I went to a church fellowship and with as much courage as I could muster, I actually ate a piece of cake. Not four pieces, not the whole thing— just one average-sized piece. Heaven didn't pause; the earth didn't tremble. In fact no one even noticed but me.

The next morning, I awoke in my own bed. My life hadn't fallen apart. I didn't feel a food binge being unleashed. Considering all the dire consequences I once thought would happen if I "gave in" to such an urge, I was braced for all-out war. By contrast, the results were almost disappointing. Life went on as normal. I got up, had my quiet time as usual, and God was still there, His presence still precious as I studied His Word and had my morning prayers. Then I went about my work and took care of my family and other responsibilities as if nothing of any importance had happened at all.

Did my eating habits change that day? Not really. Did I begin shoveling huge amounts of gooey, sugary desserts into my mouth every chance I got? Nope. That was ten years ago, and as far as I can honestly remember, there's never been even a single food binge since that day.

What happened to me was that I got a good lesson in what it means to be a disciplined person. I *am* a disciplined person, overall. Food isn't any different. Eating isn't any more undisciplined for me than anything else is. I get hungry; I eat. End of story. Or is it?

I wish this new attitude were as simple to follow as it is to explain. I was so used to deprivation and legalistic rules about what food I could and couldn't eat that it was hard to walk in freedom. Hard not to give in to the thought, *Now you've done it. You might as well go whole hog. You've had one piece; you could eat the entire bag and it wouldn't matter now.*

It's been hard to walk in disciplined freedom without writing down every morsel. And it's certainly been harder knowing the Bible says I'll be held accountable for what I've done in my body as well as to my body. Somehow keeping a food journal seemed necessary to be able to justify or support myself, you know, just in case God didn't believe that I hadn't overeaten. It was most difficult to accept the fact that God trusted me to be disciplined. That He knew my body better than I did and knew how hard it was for me to lose weight and keep it off. It was revolutionary for me to discover that I was acceptable to Him—no matter what.

Time to Be Free

God wanted me to be free from *all* bondage, no matter what form that bondage took: food diaries, calorie counting, food binges, carelessness, recklessness. God wanted me liberated from all those things. Disciplined freedom is His plan for me now.

The calorie counting has done its work. I've been educated by it. I know what's in food, I know the dangers of overdoing sugar, I know how many fat grams are in cheeses and meats, and I know how to select the right amount and choices of fresh vegetables and fruit. Now it's time to walk it out. Without regard to my weight, I'm being challenged to walk in Holy Spirit-led obedience. I know what and how to eat. Now it's time to be free.

Time and time again I've blown it. Not in overindulgence, as I once feared I might. No, I failed in not believing that this freedom was actually coming from God, or that it wasn't getting out of hand. When that happened I got out my calorie sheets and checked my food intake. Even when I thought I was eating in obedience, I didn't trust myself, and I really didn't trust God. I felt like the children of Israel when they wanted to go back to Egypt rather than go on into uncharted territory with God's leading. I struggled. Could I just keep a food sheet once a week? Once a month? Just to be sure?

Know what happened? I couldn't do it. God's grace and help were no longer there. If I was going to count calories after all those years of learning to walk in disciplined freedom, I'd have to do it in my own strength. Recently I described this to a friend. "God simply didn't grace it anymore," I said. "I felt like a fourth-grader trying to re-enter first grade and He wouldn't let me do it."

Trust Me, I had heard God whisper into my struggling soul. *Believe that I want the best for you.*

Next I was drawn to diet articles. I bought diet books. "Research," I told God. "Just to keep up on what's new." I was clutching at straws. I knew it. He knew it. Twenty years ago I had partnered in writing one of the all-time bestselling Christian diet books ever. It was nearly impossible to trust myself enough to leave it behind. But God was trying to lead me into something *more.* Something I considered quite risky, something bold. Something almost—well, outlandish, even crazy. And I had to admit I was afraid.

Now, looking back over this decade of learning, I can see I have had short seasons of failure and frustration. But I have also had longer seasons of victory and freedom. So what do I do when I find myself slipping in my trust and wanting to go back to keeping food sheets again? I pray. As simple as that. I seek the Lord.

Do I ever consult calorie books now? Yes, I do. Whenever I'm trying to "de-calorize" a recipe or make a favorite family dish more "heart-happy," I consult calorie counters as reference books. Using the information I find there, I substitute, cut down, or eliminate certain ingredients. I figure it all out, measure what a serving looks like, calculate how that serving fits into an entire day's meal planning, then go on from there.

Praise the Lord ... and Pass the Olives

Do you think it's easier going to a banquet buffet now? Think again. Before, I used to pray that there would be something there I could eat. Now I realize there is *nothing* there I *can't* eat. That I'm free to eat whatever is there.

But the whole truth is, I'm also free *not* to eat anything I choose. Slowly I discovered a center of control that had only been talked about before. A center of *self-control* that I only dreamed of in the old dieting days. I can't tell you the power I feel when I garnish my plate with *one or two* olives. When I take just a "smidgen" of margarine or add a *hint* of gravy. Before, it was either no olives at all (and a generous portion of pride) or a handful (with an unbearable load of guilt). It was no margarine whatsoever or scooping it up by the spoonful. And gravy? Oh, no, I would never eat gravy in my dieting days! (Except on those occasions when I ladled it on rebelliously.) So you see, this kind of control—balanced self-control—was totally new to me. Exciting and scary, but for the most part more than wonderful.

To me, the most unreal part of my entire story is this:

Except for being large, *I feel absolutely normal.* And within the last few years, I've even begun occasionally to feel normally large. But out of control? Gluttonous? Bingeing? Nope. Not at all.

Do I ever overeat? Probably, although I can't remember when I've done so. I don't overeat regularly—certainly not as much as I did when I was dieting. There's just no need for it anymore. I eat when I'm hungry, stop when I'm full. For the most part I choose healthy, wholesome foods. I eat marvelous fresh vegetables and luscious fruits. I choose whole-grain breads and low-fat whole-grain crackers. But the most miraculous thing of all is—I eat without guilt.

Treat Yourself ... Without Guilt

Not long ago, I was treated to a fabulous dinner by my editor, along with a couple of other people. I planned ahead of time to choose beef. I watch the amount of beef I eat on a regular basis, and since it is one of my favorite main courses when eating at wonderful, high-class restaurants, I "fasted" beef for an entire week. Then, as my editor's guest, I relished it without guilt.

Later, the dessert tray, laden with all kinds of "decadent" cheesecakes and other confections, was brought for the examination of the women at my table. "Oohs" and "aahs" were predictably mixed with the usual, "I shouldn't. I mustn't. Well, maybe just this once."

But me? I had another plan. I have learned that if you go to a large, well-known restaurant, they often have some of the best European sorbet imaginable. It's usually not on the dessert tray. I shook my head at all the rest, ordered the sorbet, and, sure enough, it was out of this world. Had I been dieting, I would have skipped dessert altogether or joined my "just this once" friends with the most fat-laden dessert on the tray. Hey, fat-laced desserts you can find anywhere. But the finest European sorbet? That's a rare treat not to be missed.

So, what am I saying? Just this: Once I decided to accept my body, I began to think more highly of it. The respect for how my body has taken the punishment I have given it and continued to serve me day after day helps me to appreciate how much I need to give it every chance to be healthy and well cared for—even at this size. I refuse to destroy it. Not with overeating and not with dangerous dieting obsessions. Not any longer.

And what about my size? My freedom and health have become more important to me than my size. Discipline is my priority, balance my goal. I choose order in all of my behaviors, habits, and attitudes, especially eating and dieting. Living large, loving myself, "even though."

The Dangers of Disordered Eating

Next I took another look at overweight women and their eating habits from a totally new, more realistic perspective. It isn't only fat women who struggle with their weight, of course. There are many women who suffer from "disordered eating." Their eating habits do not reflect a desire to get thin so much as a drive not to get any fatter!

The Bulimia Battle

The clinical stereotype of a bulimic is a woman, usually a young woman, who keeps her weight down through binge/purge practices. I've met more than a handful of slim women who suffer from the practice of bulimia. I've counseled and loved many of them through this most vicious and unrelenting eating disorder. However, no one really mentions the larger woman who keeps her weight where it is through the same destructive practices.

I began to meet some of these women more than a dozen years ago. Dieting, losing barely a fraction of an ounce at a time, they live in a sense of dreaded failure. Yelled at by their doctors and their own husbands, in desperation they know what to do before the next weigh-in. I've heard the stories, and so have you, of the women who attend a weight group together, perhaps even in their church. Afterward they all breathe a sigh of relief and head for the nearest pizza, pie, or ice cream shop. After all, they have an entire week to starve themselves for the next scale-encounter. Binge, starve. Binge, purge. And don't forget the water pills on the day of the meeting.

All part of the same monster? I suspect so.

Anorexia Nervosa: Power Struggle to the Death

"The diet took hold of me," one woman wrote. "All day I thought about food. I wanted to eat, but even more, I wanted to keep losing weight. I wanted to get thinner."[2] This statement made by a person diagnosed with the self-starvation eating disorder anorexia nervosa could have been made by me and millions of other weight-loss and diet addicts. It's not the first time the similarities have come to my attention.

"Anorexics realize the power food has over people," says Vivian Meehan, founder and president of the National Association of Anorexia Nervosa and Associated Disorders (ANAD). "A person who starves himself thinks he is special because he can do something no one else can do." Power is a major issue with anorexics.[3]

That's not an issue exclusive to anorexics, my friends. Do you remember taking off forty or more pounds and feeling extra special, extra pleasing? I do. Can you identify someone right now who has recently dropped a lot of weight who is obnoxious and exudes superiority? I can.

And there are other similarities.

Low Self-Esteem. Low self-esteem and feelings of being ineffective are common to both overweight women and anorexics. Perfectionists, overachievers, obsessors, and even enormously self-disciplined individuals can be found in both groups. Failure, hopelessness, and doom are daily companions.

"I can't do it again," one attractive woman said, tears running down her cheeks. "I did it once, and for all that I have inside me that wants to do it again—I can't. I just can't. I made it to *thin*," she said, "but I never made it to *free!*" Loving the attention she got from friends and family as she lost weight, she felt invisible as she painfully regained all she had lost and more. "It's not even what they say," she cried. "It's more what they *don't* say that hurts so much."

Hypersensitivity to criticism. Are the ultra-thin anorexics the only women who are typically hypersensitive to criticism, particularly about their appearance or weight? Not on your life. Many overweight women are too. And, like their skeletal sisters, they are also distrustful of health-care professionals, more than anyone else can possibly even know or understand.

"I can't go back," one large woman said, choking back her pain. "The doctor wanted to put me on the new diet pills and even wrote me a prescription. He'll never understand why I didn't even get the prescription filled. And," she added, "I certainly don't want to start all over again with a new doctor."

Feelings of worthlessness. Anorexic people live with the fear that they are undeserving to take up space, not worth anything to anybody, a typical finding of Peggy Claude-Pierre, who established a controversial center for treating acute and critical cases of the eating disorder. Peggy hugs, cajoles, and encourages her patients back to health. Convinced that anorexia is an attempt at suicide that is unconsciously motivated by frustrated perfectionism and feelings of worthlessness,[4] she helps her patients feel valued and worthwhile.

I first saw Peggy's story on television. I watched through tears as she rocked a grown woman and spoke reassuring words of value and love to her. *Dear Lord,* I prayed silently as I watched, *I know exactly how worthless and devalued that woman feels.*

Actually I'm not that different from the woman who was crying on Peggy's shoulder. Except for the weight, that is. Inside I have felt the exact same feelings of frustration with my inability to look like the perfectionistic ideal I held out for myself for years. I know exactly how it feels to live day in and day out feeling like a total failure, fearing that I was undeserving to take up space, not worth anything to anybody. Not to God, not to my family or church—and certainly not to myself.

Similar, Yet Different

Yet, for all the ways that overweight people are like anorexics, we're not the same. I can't actually or even experientially compare the pain and danger of such a critical illness as anorexia nervosa to the pain of being overweight. I do, however, recognize many of the fears and frustrations as my own.

It was an abrupt eye-opener when I realized that I had been more motivated to change my body size than to live disciplined but free. This was a pain-filled but freeing realization for me. I saw that I was only willing to let God be in charge when I thought there was something (thinness) in it for me. I wondered about others as well.

Going through my files of letters from my readers, I found many comments that I had missed earlier.

"Please, help me," one woman wrote. "God has been dealing with me about my weight. I'm up to 150 pounds! At fifty years old I look more like my mother than I do myself!"

"What shall I do?" another lady asked. "At a size 16 I look awful! How can I ever tell anyone about Christ until I take this disgusting body back down to a size 10?"

And there were more:

"Please pray for me. I can't stand to have marital relations with my husband anymore. He's such a dear man and he hasn't said anything to me about it, but I know what he's thinking. With this extra thirty-five pounds, I know what a disappointment I am to him. If God doesn't help me lose weight, I think I might lose my husband. He certainly deserves better than this."

"I'm writing because I want to be pleasing to God. I think He wants me to go on a 500-calorie limit each day. I know with His help and strength I can do it. I hate myself for getting this fat."

Not one of the letters I found in my files said anything like, "I'm writing to ask your help. I've discovered that I'm out of control in my eating and believe I'm doing harm to this wonderful body that God has so graciously gifted me with. Can you help me be more of a blessing to myself in this regard?" Nor did I get a letter that said, "God has really been dealing with me about the way I've been hating my body. Can you help me regain a balanced view of the physical body and how I can be a better steward of it in order to serve and honor God more?"

Take Another Look

Did you recognize yourself in any of the comments above? I used to. But no longer. I don't believe that God ever intended one obsession be replaced by another. Is it God's way to free us from one bondage by addicting us to something else?

The words of Galations 3:3 have always meant something special to me; they have taken on even more meaning to me lately.

Are you so foolish? After beginning with the Spirit, are you now trying to attain your goal by human effort?

The New American Standard Bible says it like this:

Having begun by the Spirit, are you now being perfected by the flesh?

When we read Galations 5:1 we get an even clearer picture:

It is for freedom that Christ has set us free. Stand firm, then, and do not let yourselves be burdened again by a yoke of slavery.

That's why I'm taking this stand now. That's why I'm writing this book. You and I deserve more than to be bound to our weight and image obsessions one moment longer. Does it do us any actual, spiritual, or emotional good to lose weight if we end up chained to our diets? Does it help us to regain weight and end up enslaved to feelings of failure and worthlessness?

Doesn't it make more sense to *use* our dieting history as proof that we are disciplined people? Can't we take the rough road we've traveled as evidence of God's protection and support and acceptance of us at any size? What will it take to convince you that God's not mad at you for being larger than what *you'd* like to be?

Could you trust Him for the strength to be disciplined and controlled in your eating and still live large? What would change for you if you actually heard God say that you could live *your* life—your very own life—as your very own self in your very own body? Would you know how to begin? Want to find out?

*D*ear Heavenly Father, I'm seeing a new purpose for Your plan for my life: to live my own life, glorifying You in all things, just being me. Help me, Lord, as I explore this new freedom. Prompt me when I'm about to make a mistake, forgive me when I do. Show me how You see me and show me how You plan for me to live. Give me the courage to live free of obsessions with my weight, my appearance, and food. Help me walk in disciplined freedom as a responsible adult making my own decisions based on the wisdom You give me. I choose to trust You at this new level. I want to be free, free to be the person You made me to be. Amen.

And, at this point, if you're mad at me, why not add this to your prayer:

*D*ear Father, help me also to give Neva the benefit of the doubt. Help me to remain open to what You have taken her through and what she feels led to write. Father, help me (forgive, love, accept, understand— you know what you're struggling with) as I read the rest of this book. Help me to understand what You're saying to me about me. Let me see that Your love isn't size—or performance—dependent. Amen.

Section Three

LIFE AND LOVE ON A GRANDER SCALE

Chapter Six

CHOOSING LIFE!

I have set before you life and death, blessings and curses. Now choose life, so that you and your children may live and that you may love the Lord your God, listen to his voice and hold fast to him.

DEUTERONOMY 30:19-20

One of the very first biblical principles I ever wrote about was from this chapter of Deuteronomy. God's promises, proclaimed by Moses, must have sounded strange to His children who had been living in the difficult wilderness for nearly forty years and had seen their elders and beloved leaders die without ever seeing the Promised Land. Even Moses was growing older and more tired by the day.

For some of these people, who were born in the desert, the slavery experiences of Egypt were no more than stories, tales spun by their parents and grandparents. The only reality many of them had known was the hard struggle of desert life. The bright future ahead of them, of which their parents and Moses had spoken with an unmistakable sense of longing, seemed uncertain at best. Many of the wanderers really couldn't understand what they had left, much less where they were going. So they must have felt as if they had no home to return to and no place to go. All they knew was God's assurance that the promise would come in time—God's time.

The law was being given through Moses one detail at a

time. It might have seemed like he was making up the rules as they went along.

This Isn't About Thin

After my surgical reversal, every time I stepped on the doctor's scale and saw the numbers creeping upward, the words from Deuteronomy invaded my discouragement and rang with new meaning deep within my heart. I know what it feels like to have no place to return to and no sight of the promise ahead. But God's ancient words comforted me just as they had comforted Israel thousands of years ago.

This isn't about thin; it's about life. I recognized the voice of the Holy Spirit and began to repeat His admonition several times a day. *This is about life.* Over the next few years I would quote it repeatedly—sometimes through tears and many times through gritted teeth. I was determined to see this through, no matter where God would lead me, no matter what difficulty He chose to trust me with. I followed in obedience to His Word. I had chosen life, and this was the result. If I could trust Him with my life, I would trust Him with the result.

I felt personally challenged to believe that I couldn't choose life and then treat that life as if it were a curse. I knew when I chose life, even life as a *large* woman, it would be my decision and not a fate that was forced upon me. Somehow, with God's help, I determined to find joy and celebration in the fact that I chose to live large rather than die thin.

No one lives in a vacuum. Others are always affected by our choices. When I considered my choice, I had to consider my family: my husband, our three children, and the grand-children yet to come. Their lives would be forever changed, not only by *what* I would choose to do concerning my health, but also by *how* I would choose to handle the results of that choice.

Would I really choose thinness and, in all likelihood, leave my husband behind with three children to raise on his own? Or would I choose life and be around during the years ahead when he would need me more than ever?

Would I teach my daughters that regaining weight was the most terrible thing in all of life? Both in their teens, they were going through their own struggles with identity and self-worth. How I handled this difficulty would show them how a woman of God manages adversity, how a woman of faith deals with what seems to be a terrible trick of fate.

That You May Love God

In Genesis 2:7 the making of man is a vivid picture of God's creativity. In no other place does the Bible say that God gave His other handiwork His own breath. "The breath of life," the Bible says. Not just a breath of air. Can't you picture it? God holding the limp, lovely, created form in His hands then bending low and *whoosh*—mouth-to-mouth resuscitation on a divine scale. God gave man something unique, dis-tinguishable from the breath of air He gave to all the other living creatures. *The breath of life.*

When we choose life, we choose God. It's as simple as that.

I saw that I needed to cherish the breath of life. God's

miraculous breath of life gave me not only my physical life but my spiritual life.

When I chose to cherish life, I felt a deeper love for God. I began to sense a new beginning. Different, of course. I was no longer the thin, *Free to Be Thin* lady. My life now had meaning that went beyond my size, my public identity, my reputation, my work. I was becoming obedient, even to death—the death of all I had known and hoped for. The death of all I had worked for and all I thought I ever wanted. And in that obedience, even that type of death, I found new life.

As strange as it sounds, because I surrendered to God, I became willing to have my life change from all that I had known and loved. Then, even as a larger woman, I discovered new personal understanding of Matthew 7:14:

> But small is the gate and narrow the road that leads to life, and only a few find it.

The small gate? The narrow road? Maybe when I was a size 10, but now, in a size 22? Yes. It was then, as a large woman, that I experienced the narrow way: *Trust. I learned to trust God at a level I had never understood before.* I learned to trust Him with my *whole life.* Large, small, medium-sized—it no longer mattered. What mattered was that He had determined a pathway of trust and obedience for me beyond anything I had ever imagined. I was learning the lesson of Matthew 10:39; I was losing my life—only to find it again. Loving Him was the sure footing I needed if I was to survive this difficult pathway. Choosing life was my way of loving God like never before.

Listen to His Voice

Never had His voice been clearer. Directives like the one in Luke 12:22—"I tell you, do not worry about your life, what you will eat; or about your body, what you will wear"—rang in my heart like glad songs. "I'm looking at a size 2X here, Lord," I prayed one day. "But I'm not going to worry about it. Is that OK with You?"

"Life is more than food," He reminded me from Luke 12:23, "and the body more than clothes."

I read Romans 6:13 with new understanding. Without even a hint of doubt, I knew I had been brought from death to life. How could I do less than offer all the parts of my body to Him as instruments of righteousness? I prayed that my hands would be tender hands when I came in contact with those who needed a touch from God. I asked God that my hugs would be life-giving and comforting. I pledged my feet would walk where He sent me. I decided that my mouth would praise Him, no matter what my size!

Listening to His voice, I was hearing totally new things. Even when I didn't like my larger body, I loved the new things I was hearing in my heart.

Hold Fast to Him

Choosing life on that awful, terrible day in the doctor's office, I chose a type of baptism. Not the same kind of wonderful, ceremonial baptisms we hold in our church services. But a baptism of obedience. Even when immersed in pain-filled dread and hopelessness, I knew I was covered in choosing obedience to God's pathway for me. I clung tightly to my personal Lord and Savior, Jesus Christ, like never before. And like Romans 6:4 says, "We were therefore buried with him through baptism into death in order that, just as Christ was raised from the dead through the glory of the Father, we too may live a new life." Now I could choose to see death, let it overwhelm or even destroy me, or, like Christ, I could choose to see beyond this death to new life. A deeper life, a deeper calling—a closer walk, holding on to Jesus.

Holding on to Him tightly, life now promised more, not less. But it would be harder, not easier, than I could have ever imagined.

The Lord Is My Life

Is the Lord my life? Certainly when what I wanted more than everything else in all of life (to be thin) was challenged, I was forced to answer that question with total honesty. Could I let go of my most cherished dream, my hope and accomplishment? Could I give up my very life if He asked me to? Would I?

Would you?

Would I be able to insist on having my own way and then with integrity be able to say, "I 'live to God' and God alone?" I've learned to walk this phrase of Romans 6:10 every day. This isn't Neva's life I'm living now; I left that life on an operating table in Southern California. I purposely let all I knew and all I was die that day. I did it because I heard the Lord asking me to choose His life. Now that's the life I live.

Galatians 2:20 has become a reality for me. I've learned what it is to say, "I have been crucified with Christ and I no longer live, but Christ lives in me. The life I live in the body [yes, even this larger one], I live by faith in the Son of God, who loved me and gave himself for me."

And He Will Give You Many Years

For a long time, I felt as if my life was over. I thought that while everyone wanted to hear from a thin Neva Coyle, no one would want to hear this tale of woe from a fat one. He will give me many years? *Oh, please, God,* I prayed, *don't make it too many.* Heaven looked mighty good to me on many of those long days and even longer nights.

But God wanted to give me years—not years of a terrible, lonely, and hated existence but years filled with life and vibrant with meaning. Life as a large person didn't mean that my ministry was over, that my giftings had departed, or that my calling had been declared defunct. God didn't mean that my life would be filled with discouragement and despair. This was *His life* pumping through my veins. His spirit was to be the animating principle in my life.

Finally I realized that my talents, looks, or best-selling books didn't give me life—God did! My zest would come from Him. My purpose and passion would be born of Him. How could I continue to breathe God's miraculous breath of life and live disheartened, sad, and down in the mouth one moment longer?

If I had indeed obeyed Him in this decision—and I believe with every single ounce of my present weight that I did—then could I believe that He would reject me because of the result of that obedience? No, of course not. Once I finally settled that, I found peace. Peace, not only with my size, but peace with knowing I was acceptable to God regardless of my weight or size. In that peace, I renewed my commitment to belonging to Him.

Disownership, Discipleship

Do you not know that your body is a temple of the Holy Spirit, who is in you, whom you have received from God? You are not your own; you were bought at a price. Therefore honor God with your body.

1 CORINTHIANS 6:19-20

What? Are we talking about this *body, God?* I looked up from my Bible and glanced in the mirror. Surely I felt as if a thinner body would be a fitter temple for the Holy Spirit. It was far easier to believe I honored God when I had lost weight. But in this cathedral-sized body? How in the world would I ever be able to honor God with *this* body?

What I didn't see until many years later was that by choosing life I had already honored God. By choosing life, even when that meant living at a much larger size, I still held the Spirit of God within my heart and soul. Just by trusting God with my life, my unique and God-ordered life, I was pleasing Him. It had nothing to do with size. It had everything to do with surrender.

I was God's creation. His handiwork. I was destined to live the life He had given me and do the "good works" He said in Ephesians 2:10 He had prepared in advance for me to do.

The words of Ephesians 4:1 seared their way into my very inner self: "As a prisoner for the Lord, then, I urge you to live a life worthy of the calling you have received."

Choosing Life Every Day

God taught me discipline through my eating many years ago. The fruits of those lessons have helped countless thousands find help and freedom from the tyranny of overeating behaviors. Remember, this book isn't about returning to undisciplined eating. Not in the least! If you've read that in these pages so far, you've missed something. If you think I'm advocating a reversal of thought concerning the bondage of a careless and unbridled appetite, you might as well go back and begin again.

This book goes beyond anything I have ever taught before. It goes beyond eating. It goes beyond weight. In fact, it goes all the way to the cross. It's not a book about giving up something, even with God's help, to get anything else. It's about giving up ourselves and our lives—our preconceived ideas about how they should be lived and how we should look while we live them. It's about loving and following God to the ultimate—even if His requirements are far different than we once thought. It's about finding worth and purpose far beyond physical size or appearance.

This book is about life—your life, my life. Lived in glorious relationship and loving obedience to God, our Father, and in intimate relationship with His Son, Jesus Christ.

Would I know how to live a life that was totally God-determined and uniquely mine? To be frankly and brutally honest, no. Would you? I wonder.

Have we been so busy trying to fit a culturally prescribed ideal that we've lost touch with what's real? If we once stopped living for the next five-pound weight loss or the dress two sizes down, would we have a life at all?

For, you see, if we aren't living in obedience to God, wherever He may lead us or whatever He may take us through, we're still living our own lives. Perhaps even living lives imposed by others' requirements and, in our culture, even by advertising standards. When we do that, we're settling for less than being ourselves and everything God says we can be. But we don't have to do it any longer. We can be free. I am free to be me, and with God's help, you can be free too.

*D*ear God, we have been so selfish with our lives, holding them back until we thought we were perfect and suitable for You. Help us, dear Father, to know You and to experience Your love in deeper, even more life-changing ways than ever before. Forgive us for holding You at arm's distance with the arrogant attitude that we could do anything but present ourselves to You wholly, honestly, and just as we are at this very moment. We choose life, Father. We thankfully accept Your breath of life. We gratefully accept that You see far more value in us than we've been taught to see in ourselves. Give us life anew, Heavenly Father. Help us to be free. Amen.

Chapter Seven

BEAUTY IS A LOT MORE THAN SKIN-DEEP

*A*t a recent women's retreat, I shared some of the concepts of this book. At the end of my session I asked a simple question: "How many of you have let your appearance stand in the way of doing something God has called and equipped you to do?"

Out of approximately 150 ladies, nearly 50 raised their hands. Tears flowed freely. One young woman wept openly.

I'd like to say I was surprised by the response. But I wasn't. You see, I know how addicted to appearance we are. When we think our appearance is unacceptable, we back off. Our talents, gifts, and even God's call on our lives are no longer the most important. We let someone more "desirable" or "attractive" tend to the areas of service and ministry we are called to. We decide that we are unfit, disqualified— simply because of how we look.

It boils down to this one question: When appearance is everything, what is left? Only you can answer that for yourself. Maybe I can help, but you will ultimately have to make the determination to be free to be yourself, just like I determined to be free to be myself.

Over Whose Weight?

"I'm just glad you're alive," my husband has said.

"You're a lucky girl," my doctor has commented. "Considering what you've put this body through, your being in reasonably good health is close to a miracle."

But, I want to protest, *I'm unacceptable. I'm overweight!* But is that true? When you get right down to it, the question is really this: *Whose weight am I over?*

When you look at the height-weight charts, I'm clearly out of range. But when you look at the women in my family, I'm pretty normal. All the family pictures for several generations show large women. My grandmother was large until her last ten to fifteen years. She died in her nineties. My mother has been large all her life and now, in her eighties, she's getting smaller just like Grandma did. My mother dieted from time to time, my grandma didn't. Grandma did mention from time to time how important it was to "watch what you eat." She believed in being disciplined, and I can remember warnings about not "gorging yourself." But diet? Not that I can ever remember.

The interesting fact here is that although Grandma didn't diet and Mama did, it made very little difference in the long run. Their body-weight patterns are almost exactly alike. "We come from a long line of big women," my grandma used to say. "And, Honey, you're just like the rest of us."

I fought this fact for years. I didn't mind coming from a long line of big women as long as I wasn't big myself! Somehow I, along with my sisters and cousin, took on that genetic predisposition with a vengeance. And some of us ended up with a lifelong preoccupation, an obsession, with our appearance and body size. But no more of that for me. I've decided to pursue beauty another way. I'm striving for beauty apart from my appearance and size—beauty of the heart and spirit.

The Beauty of Inner Simplicity

Your beauty should not come from outward adornment, [but from] the unfading beauty of a gentle and quiet spirit, which is of great worth in God's sight. For this is the way the holy women of the past who put their hope in God used to make themselves beautiful.

1 PETER 3:3-5

When we consider our culture's present emphasis on outward appearance and when we consider the social implications we put on what makes us acceptable, we have to take another look at this scripture, don't we? Where did we get offtrack? We're supposed to focus on the inner self apart from personal presentation? Could it really be true? In a world that puts such extreme importance on externals, such thought as expressed in this passage of the Bible seems nothing short of radical.

One only has to realize how many "standing" appointments are kept at the local beauty shop each week to understand that the beauty we stress so much fades ever so quickly. Yet the Bible clearly teaches an unfading kind of beauty. An inner beauty. Not a beauty dependent on pills, shots, and weight-slimming programs. Not a beauty based on hair colors, curls, or facial treatments. Nor is such beauty to be found in aerobics classes, designer jeans, or spandex. This beauty is much simpler; it is the beauty of a gentle and quiet spirit. The ageless beauty of a pure and tender heart.

God's Word is perfectly clear: Outward beauty is of no importance while inner beauty is most important.

First Samuel 16:7 is a revelation of God's priorities. The prophet Samuel had been sent by God to anoint a new king. The last time he had been sent on such a mission, Saul was God's selection. First Samuel 9:2 says that Saul's physical appearance was most impressive. This time, however, it was different, and Samuel almost made a terrible mistake. You see, when he arrived at the house of Jesse, he saw Jesse's eldest son, Eliab. Perhaps he had a momentary flashback to the first moment he had seen Saul. Eliab was an attractive, tall young man. *Surely this must be God's choice,* Samuel assumed. Immediately God spoke to Samuel. "Do not consider his appearance or his height" (1 Sm 16:7).

How often we make the same mistake. We look at appearance. We often decide that a person fits or doesn't fit a certain role based on his or her appearance alone. But listen to the rest of what God said to Samuel: "for I have rejected him. The Lord does not look at the things man looks at. Man looks at the outward appearance, but the Lord looks at the heart." Matthew's Gospel repeats the same warning when it says, "You are like whitewashed tombs, which look beautiful on the outside but on the inside are full of dead men's bones and everything unclean" (23:27).

Now, don't get me wrong here. Let's not go to extremes and assume that everything and everyone who is beautiful is sinful and unholy. No, I don't believe that at all. But haven't we put too much emphasis on outward beauty? Haven't we been guilty of assuming that if a woman *looks* beautiful, perhaps even holy, that she is? Based on looks alone? Am I preaching that ugliness is desirable here? Not at all. What I'm saying is this: We've put far too much importance on outward appearance and far too little importance on the condition of the heart.

I recently met a wonderful woman and popular conference speaker who is a worthy and godly role model for all the women in the denomination she serves. Interested in knowing each other better, we found a moment to be alone. When we discussed the issue of appearance and body-image obsessions, she confessed something quite surprising.

"I struggle more with what I'm going to wear than with what I'm going to share. It's true," she said. "I know I will be judged first by how I look, then women will decide if they will accept what I say. I don't know how to break free of this.

"And," she continued, "I'm not sure if it's their problem or mine."

I know exactly how she feels, because I struggle with the very same issues. Whenever I sense them arising, I return to the principles of God's Word and relearn the principle that my heart is of the utmost importance to God. But still, I'm aware that my appearance is very important to *people*. It's a dilemma we all face, especially in light of Jesus' admonition to us recorded in John 7:24: "Stop judging by mere appearances, and make a right judgment."

"Fine," I want to reply. "I can do that. But what about those who are judging me?"

"Don't worry about them," someone might say. "Just go knowing that you please God. That you're right in your heart before Him."

Good advice. But ...

You see, there are always those who "take pride in what is seen rather than in what is in the heart" (2 Cor 5:12) and those who can't look beyond "the surface of things" (2 Cor 10:7). Those are the ones who need this message of freedom and liberty more than anyone else. Yet many times they are the very ones who cannot, or will not, hear this declaration of freedom at all.

It is very sad but true: For many women of our westernized world, when appearance is everything, there isn't anything else.

$\mathcal{D}$ear Heavenly Father, please look on my heart. Examine me and see if appearance or image issues are keeping me from being and doing all You have for me to be and do. Help me understand that my heart condition is more important to You than my physical appearance. Yet, dear Lord, help me find that perfect balance. Help me to be a worthy representative of what You can do in a yielded heart and a submitted life. Let Your appearance, Your likeness, reproduced in me be more important to me than my own appearance. Then, Father, let me celebrate the beauty of Your holy presence within. Amen.

Chapter Eight
GETTING CLOSE TO FREE

*S*o how did I finally do it? How did I manage to escape our culture's destructive clutches on my value and worth and accept God's love as unconditional? It wasn't easy, and if I'm to be totally honest, it's probably not completely settled even yet. However, the freedom I have found keeps me motivated to hang on to the progress I've made and to press on for even more. Safe in God's love, I've learned to ask myself the hard questions and have found the courage to look at why the fear of fat was so threatening. I have found some surprising answers.

The Terror of Rejection

My earliest childhood memories are centered around the fear of being rejected and abandoned. As far as I know, I had no concrete reason for that fear, but siblings and school playmates picked up on it and learned how to exploit it to the max. It wasn't until I was an adult that I recognized the fear for what it was. And with that recognition came the awful truth of how I had coped with it. I became an approval junkie.

Approval was my "drug of choice." It's what kept me high and happy. I worked on being the teacher's helper,

Mama's good little girl, Grandma's favorite. And the more I became what brought me approval, the less and less I was my real self. I didn't fully understand all this until I was well into adulthood.

The tragic part of approval addiction is that no matter how much approval an addicted person gets, it never really silences the voice of the inner censor. Approval addicts know the approval they are getting isn't because of who they are but what they do. Eventually, the spiral of approval addiction escalates, and it takes more and more approval to quiet the nagging inner voice of personal and self-disapproval.

One day I woke up angry. Angry at the people I thought should love me for who I was, not what I did. Angry at myself for being such a pleaser. Angry at my family and friends for letting me be a pleaser. Angry at those closest to me for not understanding why I didn't want to be a pleaser anymore. But within hours, terrified of rejection, I reverted back to being a pleaser once more and sought more ways to gain approval. Until, that is, another day when I woke up angry and the whole cycle started over again.

What a miserable life! Aggressive one minute, a doormat the next. It was a downward spiral of self-destruction, to say the least.

I was already an approval junkie when my auntie took me shopping that day so long ago. When I realized that being slim would bring me positive acclaim, my weight-loss war began. That's what I struggled with during all the years of my teens and twenties. It's what led me to have dangerous, even life-threatening, intestinal bypass surgery for weight loss.

However, God didn't leave me there. Every day I praise

Him for being faithful to me and for leading me into freedom and deliverance from approval addiction and into deep inner healing. You see, even through the difficult early years of my childhood, I have also had a heart for God and the things of the Lord. Throughout my entire life, in my most distressing moments, I have cried out to God for help and support.

Through the words of the Bible, the Lord brought many exciting biblical principles into my life and personal experience. These beautiful principles have given me the exact healing I needed not so much to save my body but my life. They provided the truth I needed for the difficult days ahead. Applying those principles has become the strength and foundation of my entire writing and speaking career and ministry. These same rock-solid principles are the ones I stand on now, knowing that in this book there is not just a *risk* of disapproval but the *certainty* of it. What a complete turnaround for an approval junkie!

For approval junkies, when thin is in—*we must be thin!* At any cost, at any risk, the price of acceptance and approval is never too high. In the church we even make it the *spiritual* thing to do. And for years we spoke of weight loss in terms of *pleasing* God. Sadly, many people make the mistake of finding their worth and value in God's kingdom in what they do and even in what they look like, neither of which is true.

Underpinnings for Upscale Women

My purpose in telling you all this is to bring you back to seeing our need for another look at our identity in Christ—

an identity not based on westernized or modern culture that changes with the fashion season but an identity founded on the eternal, unchanging Word of God.

Recently I started a Bible-study support group in my church for large women who wanted to come to terms with their size and physical appearance once and for all. These were brave women who were interested in taking a different and creative approach to this most socially distressing condition. We called ourselves "Upscale Women." It was my personal challenge to see if others would be able to step into the same freedom that I have.

We started with a few basic though quite revolutionary premises:

1. That women of any size deserve to be valued and appreciated and to know their own worth apart from their size.

2. That we all deserve a chance to be whole without demands to be smaller, trimmer, or leaner.

3. That God offers unconditional love and acceptance. The world's prejudicial view has caused us far more harm than our weight ever has.

Then we declared a truce. We made a pact of peace with our bodies, releasing our spirits and reclaiming our lives through the power of the love of Jesus Christ. We revisited five very basic biblical principles as our foundation from which to build.

1. I am loved to life—not death.

John 3:16-18: "For God so loved the world that he gave his one and only Son, that whoever believes in him shall not perish but have eternal life. For God did not send his Son into the world to condemn the world, but to save the world through him. Whoever believes in him is not condemned."

Titus 3:4-7: "When the kindness and love of God our Savior appeared, he saved us, not because of righteous things we had done, but because of his mercy. He saved us through the washing of rebirth and renewal by the Holy Spirit, whom he poured out on us generously through Jesus Christ our Savior, so that, having been justified by his grace, we might become heirs having the hope of eternal life."

2. He claims me as His own—without regard to my size.

Psalm 147:1-6: "Praise the Lord. How good it is to sing praises to our God, how pleasant and fitting to praise him! The Lord builds up Jerusalem; he gathers the exiles of Israel. He heals the brokenhearted and binds up their wounds. He determines the number of the stars and calls them each by name. Great is our Lord and mighty in power; his understanding has no limit. The Lord sustains the humble."

John 10:2-5: "The man who enters by the gate is the shepherd of his sheep. The watchman opens the gate for him, and the sheep listen to his voice. He calls his own sheep by name and leads them out. When he has brought out all his own, he goes on ahead of them, and his sheep follow him because they know his voice. But they will never follow a stranger; in fact, they will run away from him because they do not recognize a stranger's voice."

Isaiah 40:26-31: "Lift your eyes and look to the heavens: Who created all these? He who brings out the starry host one by one, and calls them each by name. Because of his great power and mighty strength, not one of them is missing. Why do you say, O Jacob, and complain, O Israel, 'My way is hidden from the Lord; my cause is disregarded by my God'? Do you not know? Have you not heard? The Lord is the everlasting God, the Creator of the ends of the earth. He will not grow tired or weary, and his understanding no one can fathom. He gives strength to the weary and increases the power of the weak. Even youths grow tired and weary, and young men stumble and fall; but those who hope in the Lord will renew their strength. They will soar on wings like eagles; they will run and not grow weary, they will walk and not be faint."

3. He redeems me—without reference to my size.

Isaiah 44:22: "I have swept away your offenses like a cloud, your sins like the morning mist. Return to me, for I have redeemed you."

4. God doesn't condemn me.

Isaiah 50:7-9: "Because the Sovereign Lord helps me, I will not be disgraced. Therefore have I set my face like flint, and I know I will not be put to shame. He who vindicates me is near. Who then will bring charges against me? Let us face each other! Who is my accuser? Let him confront me! It is the Sovereign Lord who helps me. Who is he that will condemn me?"

Romans 8:1: "Therefore, there is now no condemnation for those who are in Christ Jesus."

5. I am his delight!

Zephaniah 3:14-20: "Sing, O Daughter of Zion; shout aloud, O Israel! Be glad and rejoice with all your heart, O Daughter of Jerusalem! The Lord has taken away your punishment, he has turned back your enemy. The Lord, the King of Israel, is with you; never again will you fear any harm. On that day they will say to Jerusalem, 'Do not fear, O Zion; do not let your hands hang limp. The Lord your God is with you, he is mighty to save. He will take great delight in you, he will quiet you with his love, he will rejoice over you with singing. The sorrows for the appointed feasts I will remove from you; they are a burden and a reproach to you. At that time I will deal with all who oppressed you; I will rescue the lame and gather those who have been scattered. I will give them praise and honor in every land where they were put to shame. At that time I will gather you; at that time I will bring you home. I will give you honor and praise among all the peoples of the earth when I restore your fortunes before your very eyes,' says the Lord."

Basic Beliefs or Myths?

In our thin, appearance-obsessed culture, it's hard to believe that God loves us just as we are, isn't it? We have bought so completely into the Americanized ideal body image that we've crossed the line, making it impossible *not* to believe that God loves only those who can fit the acceptable appearance or size mold.

We probably would be able to *say* a person doesn't have to be or get thin to be saved, but do we believe it? According to the Bible, it's clear: Nothing we can do can save us. It is God's mercy and grace that make us eligible for becoming one of His children. Nothing more.

And yet ...

According to our cultural standards, we are an offense. And what offense is that? One only has to pull up behind a pickup truck with a bumper sticker that reads, "No fat chicks!" to know.

The Bible assures us, "Whoever believes in him is not condemned" (Jn 3:18). But can it really be that simple? Can we actually be freed from condemnation in reference to our size? Shouldn't our belief in God and our trust in His Word help us overcome the condemnation of the world and its values? It certainly should. My question is, why hasn't it?

Admit it: Hasn't your size also been an offense to you

personally? If the Lord says He has swept away all your offenses, wouldn't, or at least shouldn't, that change the way you look at yourself? Then why doesn't it?

In many cases, we are our own worst critics. We berate ourselves for not being thin in the first place, then for not being able to stick to a deprivation-style diet long enough to get thin, and finally for not keeping the weight off if we do manage to lose. If this has been your experience, it's time to stop and ask yourself the following questions: In what ways do I feel condemned? How have I done that or at least participated in doing that to myself? How difficult would it be to stop being or feeling condemned because of my size? To stop condemning myself? God's Word has the answers, but will I accept them?

Have you ever been oppressed because of your size? Your attempts to lose weight? A weight regain?

Let me challenge you with a thought that could revolutionize your entire life and revitalize your relationship with God. Think of this: Close your eyes and think of God taking your side in the size issue. Think of His being "mighty to save." Now, could He do that if your size never changed? Could God ever be on your side if you didn't match or meet societal pressures or appearance requirements?

Not only *could* He, my friend. He *already has* for me and for many of my friends of size.

I know; it's a whole new thought. But listen, what if God were to actually "quiet you with his love" and "rejoice over you with singing" without any kind of makeover or self-improvement effort on your part? It hardly connects with your logic up to this moment—am I right?

Who and What Are We Anyway?

In my Upscale Women class, my friends and I learned some valuable and life-giving ways to look at ourselves. We replaced the terror of rejection with the joy of acceptance. We found freedom from self-criticism and deliverance from approval addiction. We no longer see or refer to ourselves as being big or small, fat or thin. We don't view our bodies as reflective of our worth, and we've begun to see ourselves as God sees us. Not as overweight or slender, not as heavy or skinny. But loved on a grander scale.

Through tears, love, and continued prayer support we choose to look at ourselves as valuable members of the family of God. That we are women of size no longer keeps us from moving ahead in God's plan for our lives or developing our skills and gifts for His purposes and knowing His calling and claims on our hearts.

We call ourselves by new names and describe ourselves in totally new terms. And approval addictions? We've kicked the habit! You can too. The same freedom we found in the power of God's Word is available to you. We begin by learning who and what we are in Christ.

But before we go into that, let's stop and pray.

*O*ur Father in heaven, Your name is holy, and Your word is true. Thank You for the reassurance that You look at me entirely differently than does the world in which we live. Thank You that the standard You expect me to live up to is only possible by Your mercy and grace. Thank You for loving me just the way I am. Thank You that Your claim on my life and Your love for me isn't dependent on meeting some physical standard or achieving some unreachable appearance goal. Help me, dear Father, to stop being so self-critical and to enjoy Your total acceptance. I'm so glad You understand my biology and see it apart from my heart and my love for You. Help me be open to the truths of Your Word and what You say about me. Help me find my true value in You and for Your kingdom purposes. In Jesus' name, amen.

Section Four

GRACE-FULL LIVING

Chapter Nine
UPSCALE WOMEN

*S*he sat across the table from me. Barely able to hold eye contact with the other members of the group, she hung her head.

"I took phen-fen," she said softly. "And now my doctor says I have to go off it. I'm absolutely terrified that I will regain the forty-five pounds I just lost."

The full ramifications of the most popular diet-drug regimen in history had not yet hit the headlines, so it was impossible for Carolyn to know then that her doctor's decision might be saving her life. All she could see ahead were days of unchecked and uncontrollable eating with certain weight regain.

Now, here she was. Her fear of weight regain had given her the courage to do something she otherwise might never have done: join this new class of Upscale Women, which promised a safe atmosphere of acceptance, love, and validation. It was not a diet group; our publicity had made that distinction clear. It was a unique way to approach this difficult and painful problem. Tentatively we stepped alongside our new friend, eager to offer her whatever we could to help navigate the rough emotional and physical waters ahead.

A Different Attitude

As our Upscale Women group formed we took a uniquely positive approach to being large persons. Certainly our attitude of hope, acceptance, understanding, and unconditional love contrasted with the attitudes the class members were experiencing in other environments such as home, work, and even our church.

We chose an attitude of *normalcy*. We took the position that we were normal even though we were large. Furthermore, we chose to look at eating as normal. While we would take a close look at eating habits from time to time, we chose not to focus on food. We weren't trying to get thinner but to learn how to live positively as large Christian women. We also chose to accept and encourage each other in healthy lifestyle choices as being *normal* and wise for people of all sizes.

We accepted the fact that these attitudes were new. We braced ourselves with the truth that new attitudes, new thoughts, and a new sense of self-worth wouldn't come overnight. We reassured ourselves that even though the word hadn't necessarily spread to the community and culture where we lived and worked just yet, we knew the truth. We pledged to be patient with ourselves and with others and tolerant of those around us who didn't understand what we were learning.

Making a Difference

Our approach to weight issues was different from the approach of weight-loss groups, so our focus was different and so were our goals. All in all, we discovered that the whole idea made quite a difference. This group wasn't going to be the usual weight-centered ministry; that's for sure. Even the atmosphere of our classroom was different. None of us wanted to miss a single session. We had never experienced such acceptance and unconditional love based on mutual respect and understanding anywhere before. We could hardly wait for each weekly meeting!

Different Values—Valued Differently

The greatest difference we all experienced came at our second class session. In preparation for our time together, we had all read Ephesians 1:1-14. Our assignment was simply this: According to this scripture, list the twelve things you are or have in Christ. Then, as you go about your daily life, watch for every time someone or some situation tries or threatens to steal the truth of that passage from you.

What an experience we all had that week!

First, we were forced to face the fact that as large women we were not accustomed to referring to or even thinking of ourselves in any descriptive terms that didn't include a reference to our size. Second, we discovered we were not used to thinking of ourselves in terms such as those found in this passage.

Think about it. Have you thought of yourself lately in such terms as *redeemed, reclaimed, born again, blessed,* or *chosen?*

"Well, yeah, sort of." That's what we said.

But are you comfortable referring to yourself as *the praise of His glory?*

What, at this size? Looking like this? we all exclaimed mentally. We looked at each other in shock. Judy repeated the words over and over: "I am the praise of His glory." But Ephesians 1:1-14 doesn't stop there. Go on, keep reading; there are lots more of these descriptive terms.

God's possession ... marked with the promise of the Holy Spirit ... called one ... cherished ... loved ... liberated ... adopted ... heir of promise ... free.

Our first reaction upon reading these words and phrases was, *Well, maybe when I'm thin.*

Oh, really? Is that what the Bible says? It does not!

You see, if these terms were only available to those who could take off weight and keep it off, 92 to 98 percent of dieters would be doomed to a life apart from an identity in Christ. Because that's how many dieters regain lost weight. Does that make sense? Of course not.

It would also mean that there is something we can *do* to make these terms apply to us, something we can *perform* to get into God's good graces. Yet the biblical teaching is just the opposite. There is *nothing* we can do. Jesus did it all, and He did it for that very reason—that we *can't!*

Have we lost the emphasis on who we are in Christ? Have we exchanged our precious, blood-bought identities for the standard the world holds as ideal and even revered? There is quite a contrast between what the Bible says about those who belong to Christ and the message of size prejudice in both our culture and the contemporary church. Our goal in Upscale Women became simply this: to embrace what God's Word says about us—without regard to size.

Daughters of the King

With the security of our identity found in Christ (Ephesians 1:1-14), we charged ahead to see what else this important book of the Bible had to say to us as women of size. For the next five weeks, we took in the beauty of God's Word and in our new atmosphere of love and acceptance, absorbed the beautiful biblical truths deep within our thirsty souls. Without regard to size, we embraced God's Word at a new level. We let it touch our souls and give us value and hope. We delighted in the Lord and literally reveled in His love.

And we discovered something quite remarkable.

We discovered that we had been allowing our size to prevent us from experiencing the depth of relationship with Christ that is available to us according to His Word. Sadly, we also discovered that we—yes, even those of us who had served the Lord for many years—had let our size stand in the way of experiencing closeness with other Christians. So we began to treat others as if our weight weren't a problem to us—or to them. Why were we surprised when other Christians started treating us better? Could it be that *we* had been sending as many—or even more—signals of our *unacceptability* as we had been receiving?

More than once during our class time, one of us would say, "I can't believe that after all this time I'm realizing that my weight isn't as much of a problem to others as I thought."

Did our church suddenly change overnight? Did all the size prejudice immediately disappear? Probably not. But we now had a safe place. We had each other. The world and even the church didn't seem so hostile anymore. Funny how that works. Once we felt safer, we acted like we were safer. More open, people found us more approachable. Some still can't figure out what happened to us. Our response when someone asks? "It's the Lord. He's making a great deal of difference in my life."

Insiders at Last

Large people know only too well the horror of feeling like an outsider. But when we look at what the Bible said about Jews (the insiders) and the gentiles (the outsiders) we find that the "outsiders" were reconciled to God through Christ, and while they didn't become Jews they did become "insiders."

God accepted them all through the work of His Son, our Savior, Jesus Christ. Can it be any different with us? Will we be classified as excluded? Based on what? Something as superficial as the way we look? No, of course not. Jesus saw to that.

But yet ...

There is a gap between the fact that biblically we are included in the body of Christ but in many ways we are excluded by the members of the body of Christ. It can be terribly painful to realize that there is a deep chasm between what is and what ought to be. We can't do anything about our brothers' or sisters' prejudicial attitude toward us or their desire to keep those of us who don't measure up to their narrow standard at arm's length. But we can do something about our own attitudes toward ourselves. We can base our identities, our worth, and sense of belonging on what God's Word says, not on how we're treated or not treated.

We'll never be pretty enough, thin enough, or good enough if we continue basing our "include-ability" on standards apart from God's Word. What I'm saying is this: It's time we discover that God can be glorified in our lives if our appearance or size never changes an ounce. He isn't more glorified simply because we change jobs or become famous or find the right man. He isn't more glorified in a little body than in a larger one. God is glorified in the lives and hearts of people because of one simple fact: Jesus died that He might be glorified in us. Not because we are perfect but because Jesus is.

Carolyn's Miracle

"I have to leave my job," Carolyn told us one night. "Thinness is so very valued at the job where I am now. You know I've gained back twenty pounds since going off the pills." We hadn't noticed.

What we had noticed was that Carolyn had taken new interest in her appearance. Her outfits were coordinated with a little more care. Her eyes sparkled, and her red-brown hair was attractively styled.

"What will you do?" someone asked.

She named an interesting open position at a large, exclusive tourist hotel in our area. "I've already applied and have an interview tomorrow."

Surrounding her, we took the time to pray and ask God for favor and an open door. We petitioned our Father to grant Carolyn her deepest desires—then we stepped back and waited for God to answer our prayers.

You can only imagine our excitement when the next week she reported she was beginning work the very next day! Her sense of value and worth had never been higher, her outlook never more hopeful. And the twenty-pound weight regain?

"Oh, that," she commented. "I haven't thought of it in days! There's just so much good going on in my life that I haven't had time to let it get me down."

How about you? How did you react the last time you had a weight regain? Could you use a miracle in your heart and in your life like Carolyn's?

*D*ear Father, let us experience the reality of Your Word until it is more real to us than the difficulty we have experienced being large people in a thin-obsessed society. Let Your love so flow toward us that it completely overwhelms all the prejudicial poison we have bought into. Let Your work go deep within our hungry hearts and thirsty souls until we are determined to see You glorified in our lives through Your Son, our Savior, Jesus Christ. Then lead us in Your ways, we pray, to live and walk worthily of the unconditional love You shower on us. In Jesus' name, we pray. Amen.

Chapter Ten

PEACE AT THE
ULTIMATE PRICE

What I propose is nothing more than acceptance of who we are and how we look when we are being our natural selves.

Such a simple freedom.

Such peace it brings to those who can embrace it. And yet accepting ourselves is so foreign to us that we're often terrified by the thought of it. Why are we so afraid to accept ourselves just the way we are and then to walk in freedom?

Is it so terrible that I should finally declare peace with my body once and for all? That I should allow myself to express my gifts and talents without the distraction of hating how I look while doing so? Of course not, and it can be the same way for you too.

"But won't I lose all sense of self-control?" I can almost hear you asking the question. "I mean, if I walked in the freedom of self-acceptance, wouldn't I just go off the deep end and binge myself into oblivion?"

Not necessarily.

Liberty or License?

You see, *liberty* is not the same thing as taking *license*. In Christ we have liberty, yet we also have a personal responsibility and a need for accountability in the things we do. Being large is *how we look;* eating is something we *do.* For many people, being large is beyond their control. Eating, on the other hand, making responsible and healthy choices, isn't. What I'm saying is this: There is a great deal of difference between something being *beyond control* and being *out of control.*

Dieting statistics reflect this. For years many studies and countless articles have informed us that 100 percent—that is, *all*—of those who diet to lose weight can lose. However, well over nine out of ten dieters put the weight back on within two years. Why? Is it the dieter's fault or the fault of dieting?

I have come to understand that while I may be able to keep my eating under control, my weight has been beyond my control. It took years, but I have finally chosen to focus my attention on being responsible in my eating habits without regard to my weight whatsoever. I choose wisely and make healthy selections not because I hope it will make me thin but because as a responsible adult I want what's best for me and my health. In doing so, I am using my energy where I know it will do the most good—to control what I *can* control—and walking away from those things I can't.

It seems so simple, doesn't it? Then why isn't it? Why is it so hard to believe that God offers freedom and peace that doesn't require a person to alter his or her size?

Galatians 1:3-4 says, "Grace and peace to you from God

our Father and the Lord Jesus Christ, who gave himself for our sins to rescue us from the present evil age, according to the will of our God and Father."

Grace and peace? While hating our bodies and reserving self-acceptance until we manage to slim down to a size 9? Can't we accept God's grace and peace at our present size? God has always offered us grace and peace, from the very beginning. He sent His Son, Jesus Christ, to die for our sins, yes, but also for more, much more. He also died that we might be rescued from the evil of our age. It is His will that we take His peace and His grace into our hearts and our daily lives, apply it to our most troubling situations, and experience it for ourselves.

That is the basic premise on which our entire personal relationship with Christ is based. It's that simple. We were sinners, separated from God, who sent Jesus to die for us to offer us relationship with Him once again. It's not a gender thing or an ethnic issue. It's a sin problem, solved by the Savior.

But Galatians 1:6-7 goes on to say, "I am astonished that you are so quickly deserting the one who called you by the grace of Christ and are turning to a different gospel—which is really no gospel at all."

Are we in danger of repeating the same mistake as the Galatian Christians? When we think we can come closer to God simply because we have lost weight, solved some problem, or kicked some habit, we come dangerously close to adding salvation by our own effort to the work Jesus did totally alone on the cross. I have done it myself. Perhaps you have too.

It sounds confusing, but even though I accepted Christ as

my personal Savior, I *felt* quite unacceptable because of my weight. When I got rid of the weight, I *felt* much more accepting of myself and believed myself to be more acceptable, even to God. Yes, it's true. **I thought I *pleased Him more* because I was thin (something I did) rather than being made acceptable by his death in my place (something He did).** Doesn't that skate pretty close to the thin ice of "a different gospel"? From where I sit now, yes, it does. Doesn't Ephesians 2:9 say quite the opposite when it says, "not by works, so that no one can boast"?

I believe we have let in spies from the enemy's camp and allowed them to sabotage the freedom we have in Christ and make us slaves (see Gal 2:4). That somehow we have forgotten that God does not judge by external appearance (see Gal 2:6). To whom do we think the truth of Galatians 2:20-21 applies, if not to us?

> I have been crucified with Christ and I no longer live, but Christ lives in me. The life I live in the body, I live by faith in the Son of God, who loved me and gave himself for me. I do not set aside the grace of God, for if righteousness could be gained through the law, Christ died for nothing!

Free at Last—Right?

It's time you declared your freedom in Christ right along with me. It's time that we experienced for ourselves the truth of Galatians 5:1, which says:

It is for freedom that Christ has set us free. Stand firm, then, and do not let yourselves be burdened again by a yoke of slavery.

Am I taking these words out of context? Have I bent their meaning for our convenience? Not at all. The whole book of Galatians has to do with people who would rather look to some physical, outward act to assure them of their place with God than to depend on faith in God alone. Sometime you might want to read this entire book of the Bible with our culture's dieting and thinness craze in mind. And when you do, slow your reading pace a bit when you get to chapter 5, verse 13:

You, my brothers, were called to be free. But do not use your freedom to indulge the sinful nature.

And also, verses 16-18:

So I say, live by the Spirit, and you will not gratify the desires of the sinful nature. For the sinful nature desires what is contrary to the Spirit, and the Spirit what is contrary to the sinful nature. They are in conflict with each other, so that you do not do what you want. But if you are led by the Spirit, you are not under law.

And the resulting promise? You'll find it in Galatians 5:22-23:

But the fruit of the Spirit is love, joy, peace, patience, kindness, goodness, faithfulness, gentleness and self-control.

For me, that beats dieting any day. How about you? Are you ready to believe God's Word? Willing to take the Bible's promises into your daily life and let them change your attitude about yourself and even your size?

The apostle Paul concludes this book of the Bible with these wonderful words:

> May I never boast except in the cross of our Lord Jesus Christ, through which the world has been crucified to me, and I to the world. Neither circumcision nor uncircumcision means anything; what counts is a new creation. Peace and mercy to all who follow this rule.
>
> GALATIANS 6:14-16

You are a new creation. You didn't get that way by dieting, losing weight, or coloring your hair. You became a new creation because of Jesus. That's what counts. You can have peace because Jesus paid the ultimate price to give it to you. You can have the mercy you need no matter what your size or former weight-loss/weight-gain history. God accepts you because Jesus died for your sins. If He doesn't require any more than that, should you settle for anything less?

*D*ear Heavenly Father, thank You for sending Your Son, Jesus, to die in my place and pay the penalty for my sins so I can be acceptable to You. I accept His death, the same as You do, as payment in full for my sin, and I receive the peace of Christ and invite Him into my heart anew.

Thank You, Father, for accepting me just the way I am. For not requiring that I change anything about myself, including my size, in order to find peace and relationship in and with You. Teach me how to choose the way and walk of the Spirit in my habits, attitudes, and choices. Let my food choices reflect my life in the power of Your Holy Spirit.

I praise You for all You are doing and have already done in my life and for loving me even on those days when I didn't love myself or when I refused to let anyone else love me. I repent of letting my size or appearance keep me from being close to You. I choose to bless myself with self-acceptance in the same way You have accepted me—all because of Jesus. Amen.

Chapter Eleven

REDEEMED—LET US LOVE TO PROCLAIM IT!

*W*here did all this shame concerning our bodies actually begin? One only has to read the account of the creation and what has become known as "the Fall" in the Book of Genesis for the answer. The woman had been enticed, seduced, and deceived into breaking God's spoken word. Then she easily persuaded the man to do the same. When evening came and God appeared for His usual walk with those He had created for fellowship, it was then, right then, that the very first consequence of sin was felt—body shame. Read it for yourself in Genesis 3:9-10:

> The Lord God called to the man, "Where are you?"
> He answered, "I heard you in the garden, and I was afraid because I was naked; so I hid."

Trapped by the devil-serpent, man and woman disobeyed God, broke fellowship with Him, and became embarrassed about their bodies. And the devil hasn't stopped feeding us that same lie; he has been exploiting our body image ever since. All these thousands of years later, he's still whipping us about the way we look. Yet even though you and I have no reason to be ashamed about our "fearfully and wonderfully made" bodies, as Psalm 139:14 describes them, we still believe we are devalued because of our size or our appearance.

Well, I've had enough! I'm not only tired of listening to the cultural lies about my body, I'm ready to march right into the enemy's camp and take back what he stole from me. How about you?

I no longer apologize for my appearance. I'm finished with explaining my weight loss-gain history as if everybody has a God-given right to know my inner struggles. I no longer feel obligated to reveal what I eat on a regular basis and to be sorry that I don't fit some culturally determined ideal body type and size.

I no longer accept as if it were a true fact the attitude that just because I weigh more than some people I am worth less than they are. I choose to believe God's Word about me and my value, to base my beliefs on the eternal truth of the Scriptures rather than acquiesce to societal pressure. All my friends and all my friends' friends may go on diet after diet, searching in futility for the magic cure to their body-image woes, but I'm all done with it.

(By the way, I am also done with buying my clothes through the most popular large-sized women's store and catalog until they use more realistically sized models in their advertising. I've written the company a letter stating my decision and my position.)

There comes a day when enough is enough. My size does not determine my value. My worth to the kingdom of God is not based on me, my appearance, or even my talents and gifts. It's true. We get our value from someplace else. Someplace determined by God Himself.

"The Lord God Called ..."

Think of it, walking along in the garden and hearing the voice of God speaking right out loud. If that happened to you, what would be your reaction? The same as Adam's? Would you feel you had to cover your body?

I met a young woman at a retreat recently. Because she married very young and gave birth to three daughters before she was nineteen, she now is facing an empty nest at a much younger age than most of us. Not yet forty, she's planning a wedding and sending another off to college while the third daughter has found a job in a nearby city. She said something quite shocking. "My girls and I are so close, and now they are each going their own way. One day I just cried out to the Lord. I threw myself across the bed totally stripped and bare and asked God to speak to me. I wanted to be totally open and vulnerable to Him."

I hope my surprise didn't register across my face. *Stripped and bare before the Lord in prayer? On purpose? Without shame?* I've come a long way, but still ...

You Are Mine ...

How often we forget it was God who made us. He formed our very substance, designed our genes, and determined our personality traits as well as physical attributes. Perhaps we need the kind of wake-up delivered by the prophet Isaiah:

But now, this is what the Lord says—he who created you, O Jacob, he who formed you, O Israel: "Fear not, for I have redeemed you; I have summoned you by name; you are mine."

ISAIAH 43:1

Do you belong to Him? Have you accepted Jesus Christ as your personal Savior? Then cherish God's precious words along with me: "You are mine."

If you and I are ever to confront the cultural lies about our worth, we will have to saturate ourselves in the love and grace of God. Only by letting God's Word become personal and life-giving will we ever be able to be comfortable with the fact that while the westernized world may not accept us, God does.

The Sheep of His Pasture

Whose voice has sold us the bill of goods concerning our lack of worth and kingdom value based on our culture's whims and attitudes? What voice has driven us to life-threatening weight-loss attempts? And whose voice *should* we be heeding? Listen again to what Jesus said:

I tell you the truth, the man who does not enter the sheep pen by the gate, but climbs in by some other way, is a thief and a robber. The man who enters by the gate is the shepherd of his sheep. The watchman opens the gate for him, and the sheep listen to his voice. He calls his own sheep by name and leads them out. When he has brought out all his own, he goes on ahead of them, and his sheep follow him because they know his voice. But they will never follow a stranger; in fact, they will run away from him because they do not recognize a stranger's voice.

JOHN 10:1-5

Have we listened to a stranger's voice when we have been convinced that to be fat is worse than being crippled or even dead? Jesus continued:

I tell you the truth, I am the gate for the sheep. All who ever came before me were thieves and robbers, but the sheep did not listen to them. I am the gate; whoever enters through me will be saved. He will come in and go out, and find pasture. The thief comes only to steal and kill and destroy; I have come that they may have life, and have it to the full.

JOHN 10:7-10

I've accepted that life, haven't you? I accept it, love it, and live it to the full—*now*, not waiting until I'm thin. Why? Because my life's value isn't dependant on me—it's because of Jesus.

Listen to His own words:

I am the good shepherd. The good shepherd lays down his life for the sheep. The hired hand is not the shepherd who owns the sheep. So when he sees the wolf coming, he abandons the sheep and runs away. Then the wolf attacks the flock and scatters it. The man runs away because he is a hired hand and cares nothing for the sheep. I am the good shepherd; I know my sheep and my sheep know me—just as the Father knows me and I know the Father—and I lay down my life for the sheep.

JOHN 10:11-15

When was the last time you knew someone who laid down his or her life for someone else? For you?

I bring this up because you and I need the reminder of how much God values us, how much He loves us, and how much He was willing to pay. The way I look at it is this: The value of something, of anything, is pretty much determined by how much someone is willing to pay for it.

How much did Jesus pay? Did He pay only part of your ransom from sin, leaving you to pay the rest? Of course not. Did He make only a down payment on the penalty for your sinful state, and promise to pay the rest when you get thin or when you improve your appearance? Most certainly not!

Listen again to these words from 1 Corinthians 6:19:

Do you not know that your body is a temple of the Holy Spirit, who is in you?

Do you believe these words? Do you perceive your body as God's temple, even in its present condition or size? God's Word makes no exception.

Remember Isaiah 43:1? "He who created you,...he who formed you." Think of God speaking directly to you and saying that you are His cherished one, His beloved, His temple. And remember 1 Corinthians 6:19:

You are not your own.

As Christians we accept, understand, and finally appreciate the fact that we no longer belong to the sin that held us captive before Christ came into our hearts. But there's more. You see, He didn't pay the price and then turn us over to our own devices. We are not our own—we belong to Him.

You were bought at a price.

Aha! The point of this whole chapter is in these six little words from 1 Corinthians 6:20. This, my friend, determines our worth. Jesus, and Jesus alone, can decide whether we are worth anything. He alone can assign value. And He did that long ago on Calvary, dying for you and me long before we were ever born. When we were completely lost, subject to every whim of sin, out of fellowship with God, He determined that it was worth paying the ultimate price to win us back.

If you and I can ever get that through to our aching hearts and thirsty souls we will find the strength to live valued lives. Yes, even in a culture that says we're not worth hiring or even worth knowing. Jesus said something quite different, and what's more, He said it long before thin was ever in!

Therefore ...

Therefore? Is there a catch? Is there some qualifier or God-designed loophole in the rest of verse 20?

... honor God with your body.

"What? *This* body? Are you kidding?"

What other body do you have? I thought so. Just like me, you have only one. This one precious, miraculous body. Furthermore, in the same way that you have only one body with which to honor God, only you can honor Him with it.

And you can start at this very moment.

You were bought at a price; do not become slaves of men. Brothers, each man, as responsible to God, should remain in the situation God called him to.

1 CORINTHIANS 7:23-24

God has never required any of us to come to Him in any other circumstance, situation, or condition than the one we were in when He called us to Himself. He accepted us in that condition, and He goes on accepting us that way. He values us. He determined that we were worth His very life's blood. Let's honor Him in our bodies by learning to value ourselves. Let us, the redeemed of the Lord, not only say so—let us live so!

*D*ear Father, I repent for devaluing myself based solely on superficial terms. I choose to accept the worth You have for me as defined in the death of Your Son in my place.

Thank You for saving me from the clutches of sin and death. I choose to honor You by honoring the life You have given me. I choose to honor Your Word, and I believe that You loved me enough to die for me. I choose to live life to its fullest—right now, without waiting until I'm different, thinner, or prettier. Thank You for my life; thank You for my body. Thank You for living inside me and letting my body be Your temple. Be honored in me, Father. In Jesus' name, amen.

Section Five

COPING SKILLS FOR
LIFE AT LARGE

Chapter Twelve

I'M BIG—NOT SICK!

*I*f you are a large person, you understand how dreaded even a routine visit to the doctor can be. You know all about the temptation to put off treatment, or even ignore physical problems because you don't want to face the office visit. But in this chapter you are going to discover your own personal medical breakthrough!

Doctors can be just as size-prejudiced as anyone else. They, too, are products of our thin-obsessed culture. The tragedy is, such prejudice can interfere with obtaining responsible, high-quality health care.

"Women who are more than 30 percent overweight say that their doctors often berate them about their weight, act disrespectfully while examining them, misattribute health problems to their weight, and fail to follow standard medical procedures," says Dr. Jaclyn Packer. "As a result, obese women may avoid physicians for years at a time and risk endangering their personal health."[1]

In her wonderful book, *The Invisible Woman*, Charisse Goodman wrote, "Weight prejudice is predicated in large part on the false assumption that all big people are compulsive overeaters who are automatically sick and have willfully chosen to be that way, and also that this self-inflicted infirmity justifies all sorts of discrimination against them."[2]

In another book, *The Forbidden Body*, Shelley Bovey observes: "One study shows that doctors dislike fat people, and that this dislike comes from their own middle-class values rather than from their training or from any scientific basis."[3]

Ms. Bovey also writes that a survey of doctors "describes them [overweight people] as weak-willed, ugly, and awkward," and that overweight people "are expected to prove time and again that they do not possess the negative qualities which are relentlessly attributed to them."[4]

You and I both know it's not always the extra pounds we are trying to lose when we diet but the extra emotional weight dumped on us in the form of social condemnation. When that condemnation comes disguised as "professional concern," it can be unbearable.

Have you ever felt such condemnation? Whether or not anyone in the medical field wants to admit it, medical science has miles to go before it discovers all there is to know about weight. Face it: If it were a disease or a condition that could be easily altered, wouldn't we be the first to line up for treatment? But then the diet industry would be out of business within five years or less, and after all, fifty billion dollars added to our gross national product isn't anything to be sneezed at. Somebody would have to come up with some other way to "guilt us" into spending all that self-improvement money.

Perhaps you can identify with the woman who went to the doctor finally ready to submit to surgery for a possibly malignant ovarian cyst. "While we have you open," the doctor said, "have you ever considered having a stomach stapling done?" Sound incredible? Not to me. I wouldn't have believed it, but then it happened to me.

I was dying of malnutrition. My doctor said so, and the gastroenterologist confirmed it. The intestinal-bypass surgery of 1972 had to be reversed, or I was history. Doomed to die thin or live fat was the prognosis. I wept for days. I sought comfort from my family, in prayer, and from friends. Finally I made the most difficult decision of my entire adult life. As I told you earlier in this book, I chose life.

"You know," the surgeon said that awful day, "while we're in there ..."

I couldn't believe my ears. I was already dying. My hair was falling out, and my teeth were breaking off like chalk. My kidneys were producing stones, and my skin was turning to tissue paper. My lean body tissue was so compromised that exercise of even the mildest form was out of the question, and I hadn't eaten anything but tapioca pudding and mashed potatoes for weeks. And the doctor proclaiming to be able to save my life was also willing to risk it further by stapling my stomach in order to help me stay thin!

"No, thanks," I said to the kind-faced doctor. "I've had enough of surgically altering my body to be thin. Put it back the way God made it in the first place."

In retrospect, I know I made the right decision. I wouldn't have survived. I battled for my life for the next three weeks as it was. I vomited with such force that had I also had surgical staples sectioning off my stomach, I probably wouldn't have lived through it.

Can you believe it? If you're a woman of size, you probably can.

Or perhaps you can identify with the woman who was taken to the hospital following a vicious rape. "When the doctor finished the exam and taking the necessary samples he said, 'You really should lose some of that weight.' I thought he was totally out of line and his remark inappropriate, but I was in no condition to tell him so."[5]

"I've gone to doctors for minor complaints and come out suicidal," another woman said. "All because of what the doctor said to me. You know … a doctor really has the ability to make you want to die in a lot of ways, both direct and indirect. It certainly makes you never want to come back, and ultimately, if you happen to have some disease in process, that in itself can kill you."[6]

And still another woman said that she had been talked to about her weight, not by her own physician, but by her child's pediatrician! No wonder we all want to stay as far away from the doctor's office as we possibly can.

"I wanted to scream at him," Karen said. "I'm a lifetime member of Jenny Craig, and also Weight Watchers. Know how I got those 'awards'? For *temporarily* reaching a weight-loss goal. And the temporary 'feel good' that I got was totally negated by the ensuing weight gain and feelings of self-loathing and disgust."

I know how I feel when the doctor suggests yet another thing for me to try to lose weight. Suddenly he represents the entire profession that offered me improved health, increased longevity, and better psychological adjustment through a jejunoileal bypass (surgically disconnecting all but eighteen inches of my small intestine). But with thinness the procedure also delivered gall-bladder disease, thrombophlebitis, a pulmonary embolism, kidney stones, premature aging, and early menopause. The profession that promised me "normal" life as a thin person didn't prepare me for the multiple surgeries and repeated hospitalizations that life would require. This is the same profession that convinced us that fenfluramine and phentermine—the two drugs nicknamed "phen-fen"—were not only miraculous when taken in combination but also safe.

And yet we have to go to the doctor. It's a part of life, even an essential part of life. So how do we manage our medical care and health maintenance? I have come to believe and to accept that I am essentially the one who will be held accountable for what has been done in my body. Not my doctor, not my husband, not my friends or family members. Just me. Second Corinthians 5:10 says, "For we must all appear before the judgment seat of Christ, that each one may receive what is due him for the things done while in the body, whether good or bad."

When we read that along with these words from 1 Corinthians 6:19-20—"Do you not know that your body is a temple of the Holy Spirit, who is in you, whom you have received from God? You are not your own; you were bought at a price. Therefore honor God with your body"—don't we need to take pause and say, "What am I doing in this body— *to* this body?" Does endangering our health to fit a culturally acceptable ideal honor God? I don't think so!

We have a biblical responsibility to maintain our health at any size. We can't deny ourselves the health care we need because we fear a lack of respect or because if we don't agree to go on still another diet or weight-loss attempt, we could be refused the vital lifesaving help we may need. Like it or not, we need health-care providers. So you and I had better learn how to utilize their services while keeping our emotional selves intact. Perhaps my experiences can help.

Getting Ready to Go to the Doctor

Have I given up on going to the doctor? Certainly not. But I *have* given up something. Namely this: the shame, embarrassment, intimidation, and guilt that often accompanies a doctor's office appointment. Let me tell you how I do it and how you can too.

First: Prepare yourself ahead of time with the truth of God's Word.
Several days before your appointment, read chapters 8, 9, and 10 of this book again. Let the truth of your worth to God soak deep within your spirit. Then begin to quote your favorite scriptures of hope and comfort. Find some new verses to memorize that have to do with God's faithfulness, love, and reassurance. Let the passages like the ones I've included below wash away your doubt, and let a sense of victory rise within your heart.

> You give me your shield of victory, and your right hand sustains me; you stoop down to make me great.
>
> PSALM 18:35

> Have mercy on me, O God, have mercy on me, for in you my soul takes refuge. I will take refuge in the shadow of your wings until the disaster has passed.
>
> PSALM 57:1

> Yet the Lord longs to be gracious to you; he rises to show you compassion. For the Lord is a God of justice. Blessed are all who wait for him!
>
> ISAIAH 30:18

> So do not fear, for I am with you; do not be dismayed, for I am your God. I will strengthen you and help you; I will uphold you with my righteous right hand. All who rage against you will surely be ashamed and disgraced;

those who oppose you will be as nothing and perish. Though you search for your enemies, you will not find them. Those who wage war against you will be as nothing at all. For I am the Lord, your God, who takes hold of your right hand and says to you, Do not fear; I will help you.

Isaiah 41:10-13

Even to your old age and gray hairs I am he, I am he who will sustain you. I have made you and I will carry you; I will sustain you and I will rescue you.

Isaiah 46:4

Surely he took up our infirmities and carried our sorrows, yet we considered him stricken by God, smitten by him, and afflicted. But he was pierced for our transgressions, he was crushed for our iniquities; the punishment that brought us peace was upon him, and by his wounds we are healed.

Isaiah 53:4-5

On that day they will say to Jerusalem, "Do not fear, O Zion; do not let your hands hang limp. The Lord your God is with you, he is mighty to save. He will take great delight in you, he will quiet you with his love, he will rejoice over you with singing. The sorrows for the appointed feasts I will remove from you; they are a burden and a reproach to you. At that time I will deal with all who oppressed you; I will rescue the lame and gather those who have been scattered. I will give them praise and honor in every land where they were put to shame."

Zephaniah 3:16-19

God has said, "Never will I leave you; never will I forsake you." So we say with confidence, "The Lord is my helper; I will not be afraid. What can man do to me?"

HEBREWS 13:5-6

Second: Pray for your doctor.
Physicians have been trained to treat illness. If you define your largeness like an illness, as the cause of all your physical problems, you can be certain your doctor will too. Pray for God to give him or her sight beyond your size. Pray for wisdom. Pray for your doctor's patience and pray for his or her salvation. Pray and expect God to give you favor with your doctor. It's not uncommon for a nurse to tell me that I'm the doctor's favorite patient. Why? Is it because I'm such a wonderful patient? Not at all. It's because I pray and ask God for favor with my health-care providers. I pray, and I believe I will receive what I ask for.

Third: Become your own best advocate.
When I went to a doctor for the first time after a relocation, I simply stated to the nurse that I would only weigh in after I saw the doctor. "I'm sorry," I said, "I know this is a break in your routine, but I must insist. I'll see the doctor first."

She politely escorted me to an examining room. Once behind the closed door, I nearly collapsed. I hadn't realized how much courage and strength that simple act would take. I calmed myself down and waited nervously for the doctor.

After a polite greeting and some initial information exchange, I told him of my weight-loss attempts and my surgical history. He listened with patient attention. I explained that since he was assigned to be my doctor he needed to know that I was not interested in weight lectures. That I wanted to be able to come to him without going through the trauma the scale still represented to me. (By this time I was also crying.) Then I said that when my weight was essential to health decisions or medication dosages, I would be glad to weigh in. But not as a matter of simple routine.

He listened then looked me straight in the eye. "You made the right decision," he said as he thrust his hand in my direction. "I want to congratulate you on the courage it must have taken to go through what you have. I'm glad," he said as he shook my hand, "that you are alive. According to your history, it seems you had every known side effect to the weight reduction surgery except one."

"One?" I laughed nervously. "I thought I had them all. Which one?"

"Death," he said soberly. "Death."

Fourth: Don't expect your doctor to fully understand what it feels like to be large.
Nobody else has had your experiences. People who have been thin all their lives, even if they have a large mother, aunt, or sister, can't possibly know the depth of the pain you have endured. The disappointment of lost weight, regained weight, and further difficult weight loss and rebounds can only be fully comprehended by those of us who have been there. Therefore, you alone know how important it is that you be protected and spared further insult and injury.

Before I had my surgical reversal, the surgeon assured me he knew everything about the surgery he was about to perform. He knew just how long it would take, what approach he would use, where he would make the incision, how long it would be, how he would cut and resection my small intestine, and all the other necessary technical information. He could even predict, barring complications, how I would respond after the surgery and what pain I would most likely endure.

"But," I protested, "have you ever had the surgery yourself?"

"No, of course not," he said.

"Then you don't know all there is to know, do you? You don't know how it feels."

Furthermore, he had never been fat a day in his life. How could he anticipate the emotional pain I would face? He couldn't. And it would have been unfair for me to expect it of him. Doctors have only so much understanding. We have to provide the rest for ourselves.

Fifth: Let God use you to sensitize your doctor to the needs of large people.

While being large does present a need, it doesn't necessarily represent disease. Dr. William Bennett has said that there is a modern tendency to regard fatness as a disease. "And," he added, "the result has been physiological, emotional, and moral disaster." You see, "unlike most 'sick' people, who get some benefit from the presumption of innocence that goes with having a disease, fat people have been subjected to a guilt trip because they have a 'disease' with a 'cure' that doesn't happen to work for them. Yet, instead of seriously reexamining the theory and exploring the possibility that the story is more complex than a simple balance of calories in and calories out, health professionals have been inclined to stick with their theory and their cure"—even though it doesn't prove out or work.[7]

Lynn Meletche, a registered nurse, offers these words of wisdom: "We must not continue to delay taking care of our bodies and our health. As fat people, we are often neglected or abused by the health care community. It seems as if no one wants to look at our fat, or touch it, or deal with us if we're fat, unless, of course, we want to spend big bucks with them to lose fifty to one hundred pounds first; then they may consider addressing our other issues."[8]

Once it became necessary for me to see my doctor for a long-standing stubborn viral infection. Without even looking at me, he checked my chart and inquired, "So, how's the weight doing today?"

Suddenly I found myself saying, "I'm big and I'm sick, but I'm not sick because I'm big." Yes, this was the same doctor I thought I had made contact with earlier. "I'll make you a deal," I continued. "You treat the sickness; I'll deal with the weight." He apologized, and we set about the business of finding the cause and treatment for the viral infection.

Sixth: Challenge the standard of your care if necessary.
Often nurses, office workers, and others involved in your health care need a direct but gentle reminder that fat people have feelings too. "Do you have a problem treating large patients? Surely I'm not the only woman of size you see here."

"I'm a real person in here," I once said to a less-than-caring nurse. "A real person in pain."

For the first time she made eye contact with me. "I'm

sorry," she said. "I'm really sorry."

The only way to get respect is to *expect* respect.

If you can't face the scale, give yourself permission to pass it by. You can make your position known without being obnoxious or rude. "Not today," I've said. "I've got enough to deal with, thank you."

Make sure you get the right-sized blood-pressure cuff. A too-tight cuff will give a false high reading. Take the initiative and ask for it up front. This is not like squeezing into a smaller size for your daughter's wedding. This is your health—swallow your pride for your own good.

Speak up for yourself. If you suspect that your health issues are being blamed totally on your weight, you might have to go so far as to ask for the same diagnostic tests available to average-sized patients. You might even have to say something like, "I realize that my size might be a complication to the problem, but isn't there a chance it's not the cause?"

Dress for success. You are meeting a professional. By looking nice you show respect—respect for the doctor, of course, but more importantly, respect for yourself. When we show respect for ourselves, people are more likely to respect us as well. Make sure you look your best going in—and then …

If you have had horrendous experiences with small examination gowns, ask for a larger size. If you get no accommodation, go to a medical-supply store and buy your own. They are usually less than twelve dollars. Only once did I have to bring my own. "I haven't seen these gowns before," my doctor said.

"I don't wonder," I responded. "It's mine."

"You don't have to bring your own gown," he said with surprise.

"If I want one that fits, I do."

"I'll remedy that," he said, making a note. "I guarantee it."

If absolutely necessary, be ready to stand up to a weight-prejudiced health-care provider. If you have to, challenge the doctor with the facts. Ask if he or she has read recent issues of professional journals that report the current studies concerning weight loss, overeating, and obesity. Stress how important it is for you to have a doctor who makes it a priority to keep up with recent research. For example:

The reality is this: Research shows that fat people don't eat more than thin people. Research shows that fat people gain more if they eat excessively than do thin people (many of whom overeat with regularity). Research shows that when normally fat people and thin people undereat, fat people lose less. We have greatly overestimated the number of fat people who are actually overeating. But this research doesn't seem to discourage anyone from making judgments to the contrary.[9]

Ask if your doctor has ever heard of The Healthy Weight Journal, which publishes the latest accurate information in the field of obesity research studies.[10]

Tell the doctor that you are aware of your weight, but that it isn't the reason for your office visit. If the relationship breaks down, ask if he or she has a problem treating overweight people. And if all else fails, ask for a referral to a more size-sensitive doctor.

You and I deserve, pay the insurance premiums for, and can require good medical care, regardless of our size. We can no longer put off medical exams or treatment based on less-than-courteous treatment from those we look to for care. Perhaps if you and I assert ourselves more, we will be able to save someone else the pain we've been through and indirectly even save a life.

"Neva," someone might want to ask, "are you still angry, bitter, and unforgiving toward the medical profession?"

Angry? Yes, perhaps I am, but with this important change: My anger is no longer focused inward, no longer eating me alive or endangering my health. My anger, in fact, has become more of a passion. It has become the passionate motivation for writing this book.

But bitter and unforgiving? I don't have time for such emotions. Bitterness and unforgiveness would do me more damage than trying to be thin ever has.

The passion I feel, the keen sense of mission I have, gives me positive energy and inner strength to dig a lot deeper, to find many more answers, and to speak out on behalf of all my sisters (and brothers) of size, persons who may be living less than what their God-given destiny offers. Living in guilt over something that is not their fault. All because of something so naturally assigned as biological variability.

You see, I have come to understand that it isn't just the doctors who keep us from getting the compassionate health care we need and deserve. Sometimes it's nothing more than a case of self-inflicted weight prejudice. I really believe that. When we start treating ourselves better, others will start treating us better too, including people who play important roles in our quality of life such as the doctors who provide us with quality health care.

---

*D*ear Father, I recognize that You are the Great Physician and that in Your plan, I sometimes need to see a medical doctor. Let me begin to see my doctor as Your servant, Lord, a servant who is sometimes imperfect in the way he or she treats me.

Help me, dear God, as I present myself and my physical needs for medical consultation; prepare the way for me, I pray. Let the light of Your love show through me to those involved with my care. Give me sensitivity to those who many times lack the sensitivity I need desperately. Give me love even for those who treat me with disrespect. Help me to find the medical answers I need, and help me leave the doctor's office secure and safe in Your love and reassurance.

Forgive me for neglecting my medical care. For skipping routine exams (yes, even mammograms) because I couldn't face the indignity of being large. I choose to find my worth in You and my dignity in being Your child. I choose to take better care of my body in honor to You, my King. In Jesus' name, Amen.

Chapter Thirteen

SURVIVING THE MINEFIELDS OF THE FAT WAR

*H*ave you ever seen a verse or passage in the Bible for absolutely the first time, even though you've read that very same passage many times before? That's what happened to Beth at our Upscale Women class when we studied Colossians 2:20-23:

> Since you died with Christ to the basic principles of this world, why, as though you still belonged to it, do you submit to its rules: "Do not handle! Do not taste! Do not touch!"? These are all destined to perish with use, because they are based on human commands and teachings. Such regulations indeed have an appearance of wisdom, with their self-imposed worship, their false humility and their harsh treatment of the body, but they lack any value in restraining sensual indulgence.

"Wow!" Beth said with wide-eyed surprise. "I never saw *that* before."

"How did I miss it?" Carolyn wondered.

"Would it have made any difference?" I asked.

"Oh, yes," Carolyn responded. "I could have saved

myself a whole lot of trouble, guilt, and ..."

"Money," Beth said, finishing Carolyn's sentence for her.

But such a simply stated biblical principle doesn't seem to make sense in our thin-obsessed culture. Why not?

The answer is painfully simple. Every woman who has ever been called "chubby" or "a fat pig," every woman who has ever been denied a relationship or passed over for a job or a ministry position based on her size comes to accept, then believe, that God's Word doesn't apply to her and her struggle. After all, in our culturally oriented church settings, she can still be treated as if she is less than female, less than human, and sadly, less than a Christian—based on her body size alone.

"America," says Charisse Goodman, "is a society that is caught fast in a state of arrested adolescence. As a result, weight prejudice has evolved into a systemic cultural poison that goes beyond the routine schoolyard taunting and casual gossip."[1] Tragically, the Christian of size doesn't find much relief in the church. Such thinking can easily be overlooked when biblical principles such as those found in Colossians 2 are not seen as applying to us. And words like these found in Romans 12:1-2 have to mean something else:

> Therefore, I urge you, brothers, in view of God's mercy, to offer your bodies as living sacrifices, holy and pleasing to God—this is your spiritual act of worship. Do not conform any longer to the pattern of this world, but be transformed by the renewing of your mind. Then you will be able to test and approve what God's will is—his good, pleasing and perfect will.

Certainly we cannot be expected to offer faulty, oversized bodies to God unless we mean to reduce them first and foremost.

Yet I challenge each and every reader of this book to do just that—to accept God's Word at face value no matter what your size or the size of those you love. Would such words of Scripture offer some relief and protection from what is viewed as "expert" weight-control advice? I hold that it would.

For the sake of my argument, consider Romans 12:1-2 again. Think of your body as belonging to God before it belonged to you. Understand that in accepting Christ Jesus as your Savior, you now give that body back to God. And that in accepting Christ, He accepts you—body and all. Just as you are, and your body just as it is. Then, as a service of your worship, could you unplug from the weight-loss propaganda being hawked in every form of print and electronic media? As worship, could you then present your body to God *as is*?

How many appetite patches, fat-magnet pills, diet teas, and Gut Busters would we buy then? How ready would we be to spend over forty dollars on a "fat-absorbing patch" illegally claiming to magically trigger fat burning, speed up metabolism, stimulate the thyroid, fight water retention, prevent muscle loss, control appetite, and maintain weight loss?

If we really believed that our bodies belonged to and were accepted by God, would we still find it necessary to spend good money just to slip knobby insoles that cause "weight loss with every step you take" into our shoes? Would we really order a herbal program that costs in excess of $150 a month and is based on the quack theory that our bodies must be detoxified for proper balance and function of digestive and enzyme systems?[2] In light of the above passages from God's Word, wouldn't we think again before investing in such schemes?

Would we really be so eager to ingest ephedrine-laced diet pills and questionable mushroom tea, or attend hypnosis seminars if we fully understood that these larger bodies of ours are acceptable offerings, suitable instruments of worship, to the God who made them in the first place?

The Appearance of Wisdom

Even without much convincing, you may be able to identify the fraudulent claims and bogus promises made by the weight-loss products I have mentioned here. They may even seem obviously deceptive to you, as they do to many others. But there's more. Sometimes what has the appearance of wisdom isn't as easy to spot.

In doing my homework for this chapter, I did a simple Internet search. All I did was key in the words "weight loss," and I let the World Wide Web do the rest. My inquiry produced 4,992,342 matches! I'm serious—4,992,342! Needless to say, I didn't read them all. But I read enough to confirm what the magazine rack at the supermarket had already told me: There is an avalanche of information presenting itself as wisdom that is nothing more than the *appearance* of wisdom. And you and I, as women of size, are the targets.

The Vulnerability

Without a full understanding of God's Word, we can be vulnerable to the thoughtless comments of people who believe they have our best interests at heart. When the comments are cloaked by a "compliment" or in spiritual-sounding jargon, we can be especially gullible. Maybe you can identify with some of these stories:

"I was waiting in the checkout line at the market," one woman said. "The lady behind me touched my sleeve and said, 'I'm glad to see you're on a diet. You would be a real knockout if you were thin. I just told my daughter how pretty you are.'"

"A guy I dated twice told me that if I lost weight I could be 'the most beautiful woman in the world,'" another woman said. "I tried to take his comment as a form of a compliment, but I couldn't work through it. I stopped seeing him."

"Are you losing weight?" an inquisitive woman asked at my church.

"No," I said. "At least I don't think so."

"Well, maybe it's just something the Lord is showing me. Something you could do if you'd try." I wanted to scream, cry, and escape all at the same time.

When this happens time and again, our resolve to accept ourselves gets worn to a frazzle. Tired of defending ourselves, we begin to second-guess our decision to stand firm and be healthy and happy as we are. *Maybe I'm just fooling myself*, we say privately. And the setup begins all over again.

"Why can't people see that we don't all come in the same size range?" Dee asks. "I want to scream that I'm fat and I'll always be fat and the world can just get over it. I'm sick of chasing the illusive dream. I'd rather live my life now, the way I am, and stop waiting for life to begin later—someday, when I can manage to be thin. I really want my life to stop revolving around how much I weigh."

Recognize Dee's anger? I do. And when that anger is left unchecked, we become vulnerable by wanting to lose weight "just to show 'em."

I also know the familiar feelings of self-preservation expressed by the woman who said, "If those around me can't accept me just as I am, then I will simply delete them from my inner circle and find those who can. Life is far too short to spend it on constantly worrying about how I look to others."

But is it that easy? I haven't found it so. Have you? Of course not. We want to be loved and to be given the right to love. Careless remarks, unsolicited comments, and TV infomercial testimonials all tell me I have to do something about my weight. That's when the "appearance of wisdom" becomes so dangerously appealing and our vulnerability saps us of common sense.

Innocently at first, we begin to browse through the ads once again. They can be found anywhere. We're not talking about scanning the classified ads buried in small print in the back of the newspaper. We can find the most remarkable claims in more than five hundred nationally circulated magazines. Claims that we can "melt fat off" while we sleep, "lose five pounds overnight," or "lose more than a pound a day without hunger."[3] Once again we flirt with the idea of trusting our health and well-being to unqualified individuals, buying unproven and sometimes downright dangerous weight-loss plans, programs, and products. In so doing, we become vulnerable to the risky world of health quackery.

Once we inquire about a specific product, our names are sold to lists of direct marketers. Perhaps you have received, as I have, what appeared to be a newspaper article with a handwritten endorsement scribbled in the margin: "Neva," the note said, "this really works. Try it!—Susie."

Susie? Susie *who?*

All of us have friends who have signed up as "distributors" for some multilevel marketing scheme. "Just call this number and listen," a friend from church urged me. "You can't believe the testimonies! It's wonderful. One lady took this and lost sixty pounds. Just call and listen."

She was right. I didn't believe it—and I didn't call. I'm smart enough to know that credible research is shared and critically reviewed. I don't believe testimonials anymore. Enough is enough. I don't believe those therapeutic claims any longer.

Fortunately the U.S. Postal Service protects us with mail fraud laws. However, private carriers like UPS and FedEx aren't yet included under those same laws. Although they are making efforts to warn consumers and have joined with other corporations to monitor and address fraudulent schemes, much work still needs to be done. Even though the Food and Drug Administration and the Federal Trade Commission have jurisdiction when fraud charges are filed, they need consumer cooperation and reports.

You and I have been conditioned to believe that when a weight-loss product or program doesn't work, it is our own fault rather than the fault of the promoter or product. Scientific-sounding words like *breakthrough, new discoveries, all-natural, safe, effective,* and *proven* convince us to try one more product, one more time. Even though our common sense is trying to tell us otherwise, it is easy to command it to sit quietly in the corner while we suspend our better judgment. "Well," we tell ourselves, "maybe it'll work...." And if not? "Well, what can it hurt?" But before we assume the blame for gullibly believing such "wisdom" is solely based on being fat, consider this:

At a study conducted at MIT, students were given an assignment called "Modern Times: Anthropology of Truths Project." In that assignment, students reviewed recent articles on the newest prescription diet pills. One student, Robert, selected an article in *Fortune* magazine titled, "New Weapons in the War on Fat."[4] In his report Robert said that in order to search out answers to the questions the article raised, "I would have to speak to people in very high positions in certain hierarchies of industry and government. I would probably not have the power to get that information."

"Hey, Robert," I wanted to say when I read his remarks, "welcome to my world." Then the young man went on to say:

> Those who are overweight don't seem to have a representative, but those who are of normal weight have the medical community to represent them by stating what normal is. The National Institute of Health and the FDA ... clearly state that what is defined as overweight is unclear

to biomedicine, but some "law of the land" still manages to label people overweight.

This source definitely seems to have a conspiracy-type mood to it. It tries to let the reader understand that not much is known about the upcoming "fat drugs" but to show some of the results, while announcing all of the side-effects and consequences. It seems as though the community is trying to hide those consequences, and the paper is revealing them to all.

"If I were overweight," this average-sized student went on to say, "I might be influenced more by the paper to attempt such drugs, even though I would be aware of the consequences."

Another article he reviewed from *Time*[5] left him thinking, "According to the claims made in the article, if I were overweight, I would want to try those revolutionary drugs and fool myself into thinking that the side effects would not affect me."[6]

No other non-overweight person has ever gotten closer to my mind-set than this bright student. I know exactly what it is to "fool myself into thinking" what the promoter wants me to think: that I can be thin, after all.

When we are presented with *an appearance of wisdom* and connect it to a lifelong struggle to fit into a thin-obsessed world, it isn't a far stretch to think that even Christians can fool themselves into thinking that the claims are true or that potential side effects certainly wouldn't affect them. I did, and I wasn't alone.

The Wall Street Journal reported that in the first five months alone, more than 1.2 million prescriptions for

Redux were written. That was very good news for the drug's marketer, American Home Products Corporation, who raked in a healthy share of the more than twenty million dollars a month spent on the drug.[7]

Andrea believed the claims and convinced herself the side effects wouldn't affect her. She was wrong. Taking Pondimin, also distributed by American Home Products, she lost twenty-eight pounds but developed pulmonary hypertension. "Without medication," she said regretfully, "my doctors say I have a life expectancy of only two years." Was it worth suspending her better judgment in hope that she would be thin? Andrea says it wasn't.[8]

And it isn't just our hearts that are threatened. Now there's even talk of irreversible brain damage as well.[9] Have we learned? Believing in self-made wisdom can be deadly. The well-worded advertisements from lawyers all over the country in every major newspaper indicate how widespread the problem may be. Class-action lawsuits are already pending. Hoodwinked by science? Made vulnerable by the westernized world's long-standing appetite for easy solutions to weight problems? Maybe so. But now will we be exploited by lawyers as well?

Furthermore, will you and I be forgotten in all this? Of course not. Certainly there are already "safe and effective alternatives" being offered. All one has to do is open the mailbox and browse through a mass-marketer's vitamin catalog to know what I'm saying is true.

You and I can no longer afford to believe such schemes showing the *appearance of wisdom*. How about it? Have you had enough of submitting to the basic principles of this world? I have! Even credible research tells us that we're genetically different.[10] Distinguished doctors like Michael Wientraub and his colleagues at the University of Rochester agree.

"Some force—genetic, metabolic, or whatever—must be at work, telling the body what it should weigh," Dr. Wientraub says, "and this mechanism can be perturbed for a while, but eventually [the weight] will rebound."[11]

Even the researchers from the National Center for Health Statistics in Hyattsville, Maryland said in 1994 that "a general public health recommendation for weight reduction through calorie-restricted dieting does not appear to be an effective solution."[12]

If the new diet pills can be deadly and if reducing our caloric intake isn't effective in the long haul anyway, where does this leave you and me? Where do we go from here? The sad truth is that to be a woman in this day and time is to worry about your weight—and, at the same time, to long for a normalized-eating life. Do we even know what a normalized-eating existence would be like? Can we actually be freed from the rules such as "Don't handle! Don't taste! Don't touch!"?

Could we really be at the dawn of a new attitude that doesn't actually perceive being different as defective? Is there an end in sight for the daily mental struggle to get people to see beyond our size and see us for who we really are—gifted, redeemed children of God? Is there hope that people will really someday see us as genuine, friendly, kind, and intelligent before they see us as large, fat, or oversized?

I firmly believe that, in Christ, we can stop feeling set up and vulnerable by our thin-oriented surroundings. That we can learn to handle people who question whether we are really being truthful, doing all we can or being our best, simply because we are women of size. I'm absolutely sure that we can learn how to eat out without keeping our guard up, afraid of hostile, judgmental onlookers and self-appointed diet monitors. It's time you and I started hoping for a world in which we feel accepted as people without feeling that people assume we are stupid because we are larger than they are.

We can once again become women who love to go places, do things, and meet new people. It is time to bring an end to the struggle that makes our weight issues permeate every aspect of our lives.

"But, Neva," you ask, "can there really be a happy, fulfilled life as a Christian woman of size? Is there really a chance that this issue doesn't have to have total control over us the rest of our lives?"

Oh, yes, my friend. I'm convinced we can break the chains of cultural expectations. Otherwise I wouldn't bother with the years it has taken to plan and write this book. I wouldn't have willingly fought the spiritual warfare or risked the rejection and criticism I know this message is bound to draw to me and my work.

James 1:5 says, "If any of you lacks wisdom, he should ask God, who gives generously to all without finding fault, and it will be given to him." If ever you and I needed wisdom, it is now. Let us determine that we will turn away from those things that have only an appearance of wisdom, things that only separate us from our money and endanger our health. Let us stop blaming ourselves when these products don't work. Let us commit ourselves to God's wisdom that promotes personal worth and peace once and for all. Let us turn to Him for wisdom. Let's learn the personal, individual meaning to the words of wisdom found in the Bible. Wonderful words like these:

> Wisdom calls aloud in the street, she raises her voice in the public squares; at the head of the noisy streets she cries out, in the gateways of the city she makes her speech.... "The waywardness of the simple will kill them, and the complacency of fools will destroy them; but whoever listens to me will live in safety and be at ease, without fear of harm."
>
> PROVERBS 1:20-21, 32-33

Instead of believing the claims of every weight-loss plan, product, and prescription, let us turn our attention and our hearts toward God. Let us seek Him for wisdom and reassurance that we truly "have been raised with Christ," as Colossians 3:1 tells us, and let us truly set our hearts "on things above, where Christ is seated at the right hand of God." Let us determine that we will follow the admonition of Proverbs 3:5-6:

> Trust in the Lord with all your heart and lean not on your own understanding; in all your ways acknowledge him, and he will make your paths straight.

Then let us live our lives—our new, wisdom-filled lives in Christ—knowing His love, seeking His ways and His will concerning how we should live in safety from the empty promises made by charlatans.

As determined, wisdom-seeking Christians, let us decide:

- We will accept only reliable sources of information.

- We will develop a healthy, lifesaving skepticism about advertising claims, statements made by talk-show guests, and so-called breakthroughs.

- We will choose for ourselves healthy lifestyles and caring health-care practitioners.

- We will use wisdom and avail ourselves of doctor-ordered screening tests when appropriate. When illness strikes, we will use both self-care and professional care as needed.

- We will take an active and responsible role in our health management and maintenance.

- We will learn to be wary instead of gullible with weight-loss plans and products that lack scientific support and a plausible rationale.

- We will choose to be responsible and careful consumers of health-care products and promotions, knowing that wisdom helps us maintain responsible vigilance over our health.[13]

*D*ear Father in heaven, I choose to live my life in You and the wisdom You offer me as a follower of Christ. Let me walk free from what the world offers as wisdom, which in fact has only the appearance of wisdom. Then, Father God, give me Your wisdom. Help me treat my body with wisdom. Let me live my life in wisdom. Help me not be so vulnerable to weight-loss schemes and questionable quick-fix scams. Protect me from judging myself and shield me from the judgmental attitudes of others. And when I'm tempted to try still another plan that might turn out to endanger my health and sabotage my sense of value and worth to Your kingdom, help me turn to You first. I love You and choose to live my life focusing my attention on You and Your wise plan for my life. In Jesus' name, amen.

Chapter Fourteen

CHURCH LIFE AND THE CHRISTIAN WOMAN OF SIZE

"Have you ever heard a fat joke from the pulpit?" I asked the women in my Upscale Women class.

After the nervous chuckles tapered off, one of the women spoke. "Not only have I heard them, I can tell you when the last one was. It was three weeks ago on Sunday night."

"I heard that one too," another woman said. "But I thought it probably only bothered me."

"Well, it didn't. I wanted to crawl under the seat in front of me. The scary part is, I didn't see it coming. It caught me totally off guard."

It happens all the time, was the consensus of the group.

"But what can we do?" one woman asked. "I have to come to church."

That question and its answer merit our investigation. What can we do?

How tragic that the one place we traditionally think of as a refuge is for many of us the most dangerous place of all. Even after we have been bolstered by newfound value and rediscovered worth in God's kingdom, armed with strength and resolve to survive visits to the doctor's office, and resolutely armed against health fraud and weight-loss quackery, we still have the church to face.

Reuben Welch wrote that "the church is not the society of the congenial—it is a fellowship based on common life in Jesus. It is the will of God that the Christian life be lived in the context of a fellowship of a shared life. God has made us in such a way that we really do need each other."[1] I know that what Mr. Welch says is true, and while I know it clearly defines my need, has this been my experience? Not always. Yours?

It can be devastating to go to church needing someone to accept me just as I am, to support me and encourage me for the days and circumstances ahead, and instead of being comforted be ridiculed or hurt. I can't tell you how many times I came to church on the verge of tears, a wounded bundle of pain and hurt, needing to feel the unqualified, nonjudgmental presence of a friend, someone to communicate the care of Jesus and reassure me of His matchless love. I wanted so desperately to have someone just love me, to take a moment and simply help me carry the burdens of my life. Sometimes those burdens included being a woman of size in a thin world.

As Michael Slater said, "As Christians, we have a new life in Christ. His life within us is not to be separate from our relationships with one another. On the contrary, we are called to support these relationships in a new and better way. We need other people and are meant to encourage one another."[2]

So why doesn't this model of church life exist? For the Christian of size the reasons are many. Instead of our church relationships being based on biblical principle, secular myths about large people have come to church with us and with our friends. Let's see if we can track even a few of those myths and see how they hurt when they are interpreted in the context of church-family relationships.

Myth #1: Being overweight is a symptom of a deeper spiritual problem.

The truth is, fat people do not have any more spiritual problems than thin people. But fat people do have the added stress of being fat in a thin culture, a culture that has made its way into the church. In the past twenty years, slenderness has been touted in the church as being "more pleasing to the Lord." Living with weight prejudice is difficult enough, but when "spiritualized" in this way it causes many Christians of size to question their value to God.

Those who are judged as having deep spiritual problems are often denied their full place and potential as children of God. They are often seen as poor examples and witnesses not because of their lifestyles or their beliefs but because of their size alone. How many gifted people are being overlooked for significant positions and ministry within the church—my church and yours—because they don't fit the "ideal"?

Large women make wonderful wives, mothers, administrators, teachers, counselors, leaders, and valuable contributors to family and church life. Again, the impact of our current culture makes a devastating impact not only on the large Christian but on the church. God is no respecter of persons. Christians, however, can hardly say the same.

Isn't it true that in Christ we live and move and have our being? When did the church's true measure of the quality of a Christian become his or her body size?

Myth #2: Large people are more than likely overeaters.
Since the early to mid-eighties, studies of the eating habits
of North Americans have indicated that as a group, large
people do not eat more than thin people. Furthermore,
such studies have also indicated that as a whole, fat people
may in fact be consuming *less* than thin people.

Make your own observations. Next time you attend a
church dinner, notice how much thin people eat. Notice
how we are probably more inclined to give them the benefit of the doubt. "Oh, well," we are apt to say in excusing
them, "they probably haven't eaten much all day." Or it's
very possible that we wouldn't think of anything to say
about what they do or don't eat. Why? Because it is of no
concern. What thin people eat is of no particular notice or
interest.

While gluttony is a sin, is there evidence to prove that fat
people are any more gluttonous than our thin friends with
faster metabolisms? Fat people are not always overeaters,
and while it's almost never addressed, overeaters are not always fat. Until we separate the eating and weight issues,
true gluttony will never be addressed correctly.

Myth #3: Fat people are simply rebellious.
Overweight people may at times *seem* more rebellious than
thin people, but it isn't necessarily true. Perhaps what is
perceived as rebellion is nothing more than anger at being
expected to fit into the smaller, idealized body size deemed
important and essential as an American Christian.

In my twenty years of experience in Bible-based weight-
control ministry, I've been astonished at the numbers of
large people who define *themselves* as rebellious when they

can't maintain diets of fewer than one thousand calories a day for more than a brief period. Yet all other evidence in their lives proves otherwise. Would a rebel try again and again to live at a level of deprivation required and expected of no one else? Would a rebel sob in repentance over a single cupcake or berate him- or herself for a second helping of mashed potatoes?

A rebellious person is someone fraught with and controlled by an inner defiance against any authority or control. Yet I have actually seen little of this in my two decades of ministry to overweight people. On the contrary, I have seen guilt-ridden people, unable to bear the incredible load of self-inflicted deprivation and hunger of low-calorie dieting, who give up on themselves rather than give up on the diet. Who demand impossible discipline of themselves then call themselves rebellious when they can't meet that demand. They're perfectionists but not defiant—dear people who love God and believe the rebellion myth and are sure they have disappointed Him and discredited the church. Neither of which is true.

Myth #4: Large people have more unresolved emotional issues and problems than those who are thin.
This simply isn't true. Large people do have emotional and unresolved personal problems. But more than thin people? Certainly not. There are, however, added emotional stresses simply from being large and facing weight prejudice day in and day out. But it is highly unlikely that large people have any more unresolved emotional problems than thinner people.

Being fat is simply not safe in our westernized church. It

makes you a vulnerable target of rude remarks and discrimination. It singles you out for jokes and unsolicited comments from the most unexpected places. Being large means you are often treated as invisible in the secular world, but it also happens in the church. It is true that you can be overlooked for positions of ministry based solely on size, regardless of your ability or qualifications. If you are hurt by it (because those in the church often view your weight as your own fault), you can be considered emotionally unstable and unforgiving.

Faced with the ongoing onslaught of fat-phobia, the large person either gives in and becomes emotionally wounded or learns to handle such pressures and becomes emotionally stronger. In other words, to survive as a large person, it takes an enormous amount of inner strength to stay mentally, emotionally, and spiritually healthy in spite of the opinions and prejudices of those around us.

A positive sense of self-worth is a tremendous challenge for women of all sizes. Fearing that fat would end their value, thin women often depend on unhealthy, sometimes dangerous methods to make sure they keep their thin, acceptable bodies. Christian women aren't any different. But in the church, we should be alarmed that the foundation for our emotional well-being is based on something as individual (and superficial) as the reading on our bathroom scale. Considering how much verbal and spiritual abuse is leveled at the fat Christian, it's a miracle that more of us haven't become shrill, obnoxious, mean, and overbearing. And if fat women are more likely to be depressed or lonely, it's probably because we forget that life isn't any more perfect for thin women than it is for "imperfect" large ones.

Do large people have more unresolved emotional issues and problems than those who are thin? Considering the stress of being overweight and the uphill battle to maintain not only our emotional but also our spiritual health and individual worth, those of us who can be called Christian "women of size" are quite possibly more stable both emotionally and spiritually than those we share the pew with each week.

Myth #5: Fat Christian women probably have a personal history of abuse and are more likely to have been victims of incest or molestation.

Probably not. Not every person unfortunate enough to have endured such torture at the hands of another gets fat. I've never been a victim of physical abuse, molestation, or incest—yet I'm fat. To say that a woman's size is based on her painful past is totally unfair to thin people who have pain-filled pasts. To assume that molestation and abuse result in fatness is to say to all abused, molested thin people that it couldn't have been that bad or they would have gotten fat. No one ever deserves to have his or her personal pain devalued and discounted in such a cruel manner.

Thin people who have been hurt at the hands of another have valid pain. Yet as long as such fat myths exist, thin, hurting people can often be overlooked and ministry opportunities missed. Thin women haven't escaped the cruelties of life any more than fat women. To think otherwise is unjust to both.

Nothing is as devastating to a woman's emotional and spiritual health than this unending battle with her genetic programming to forever starve and beat her body toward an unachievable cultural ideal. Normalcy and acceptance must begin with her own determination to be all God wants her to be. The church could help, of course, by teaching respect for all people, and by challenging Christians to disconnect from the image of the world and be transformed by the renewing of our minds. We must make it our goal to be conformed to the image of Jesus, not to the ads that feature "heroin-chic" models.

Myth #6: The large Christian is simply undisciplined. She could lose weight if she really wanted to badly enough.

Seeing fat women as simply undisciplined is evidence that the church has bought into the fat myths created by our thin-obsessed culture; such an idea is not based in fact. A thirty-three-billion-dollar (probably closer to fifty-billion-dollar) diet and weight-loss industry perpetuates this myth about fat women. The truth is, it is physiologically almost as difficult to permanently change your weight as it would be to change your height.

No one knows the painful existence of living fat in a thin world more than fat women. If they could, they would be thin. For some, living large is a nightmare that never goes away. I know no large person who would not prefer to be thinner, although I also know many who are beginning to accept their size as part of their normal life and to appreciate themselves for who they are without the forced demands to change.

Furthermore, thin people often brag about their genetic inheritance of a speedy metabolism linked to their thinness. However, many of these same thin people frown with disbelief when a large woman (or man) suggests that her inherited metabolism contributes to her size as well. Thin people cannot possibly understand the intense and well-founded fear of losing weight, gaining a disproportionate amount of supportive attention and affirmation of supposed self-imposed discipline at last, and then when the weight rebound begins, losing all that support and affirmation and receiving instead awkward silence. There is an unspoken message (based on stereotypical assumptions) that the thinner person believes the larger one has "slipped" back into old, undisciplined habits and a fattening lifestyle. Yet I can't find any supporting evidence that Christians of size are any less disciplined than thin Christians. Am I more self-destructive than my thin friends? No, I am not.

Myth #7: Large women are unappealing and less healthy than thin women.
Attractiveness is culturally relevant. One-third of American women wear above a size 14–16. They fall in love, marry, bear children, and lead normal, productive lives right alongside the rest of society. There are actually men who, if they don't prefer their women large, certainly don't mind or find them unappealing. There are even men (who are not sick, perverted, or strange) who are actually more attracted to larger women. Such attraction comes with a price, however. The same culture that would ban fat women from their beaches and buses considers such a man a traitor.

The Bible says a man must love his wife just as Christ loved the church and gave Himself up for her. The truly Christian man must grow enough to maintain a biblical standard of love and sacrifice for his wife without demands for thinness that would endanger her health and emotional as well as spiritual well-being. I've often wondered at the strength of any marriage that is dependent for its success on the body size of the wife.

"But," you might suggest, "in a thin-oriented culture, shouldn't the wife want to be a credit to her husband?"

No woman, fat or thin, should ever have to live under the pressure to be a "credit" to her husband anymore than a husband should be pressured to be a "credit" to her. Christian marriage is about partnering, completing, and living conjointly as heirs together in Christ. We are not ornamental creations but spiritual beings. Weight prejudice, however, both denies us and damages our relationships.

And God? Shouldn't we want to be a credit to Him?

There is not one verse in the entire Bible that indicates that a person offends God because of his or her physical size or appearance. Isaiah prophesied that Jesus Himself would be of no physical attraction (see chapters 52–53). The Bible also teaches that whosoever will may come and find salvation, acceptance, and love in Christ. And Psalm 139 says that we are fearfully and wonderfully made, that God was present even through our formative days when we were yet unborn. This means our substance, our genetic dispositions and influences, were not outside His control. Some of us are tall, some short, some thick, some thin; we're all miraculous variations of God's wonderful creation.

A woman's size may not matter to God and it should not matter to His church, but her spiritual qualifications do mean something. And it's time the church took notice.

Women do have more to contribute to the life of their churches than a fifty-pound weight loss. Gifted women are everywhere, and they can be a resource of strength, prayer power, and ability.

I started this chapter by relating a question asked of the women in my Upscale Women class. The question was, "Have you ever heard a fat joke from the pulpit?" It didn't surprise me that they could remember the date and time their pastors last made an unkind remark at their expense. Surprisingly, when I asked some pastors this question, they could not remember even making such remarks.

This serves as proof that the large woman isn't just invisible in the world, she is many times not seen in the church either. It happens again and again, and in my opinion, if it happens just once, it is far more frequent than it should be.

Making a Safe Place in the Church

In a conversation with my own pastor about this chapter and its contents, we discussed several survival facts a large person should remember when facing size prejudice in the church.

- Understand that the culture walks into your church in the minds and attitudes of those who attend.

- As much as we'd like it to be, the church and its people are not perfect.

- The church is what Reuben Welch described as "a fellowship based on common life in Jesus," but it is more—it is also broken.

Are we all one? No. Are we supposed to be? Yes. However, there is a large gap between what the church is supposed to be and what it really is. But be patient; we're working on it, aren't we? The church is broken because we are broken. **Just because we "got saved" didn't mean we got "fixed." That takes a little longer.** And in a broken church, it isn't safe to be real. Maybe it will be someday—and that is truly our goal—but for now, we have to settle for *places within* the church where it is safe to be real.

For example, Upscale Women is a safe place to express the discomfort as well as the challenges of being a Christian woman of size. It isn't necessarily safe, nor is it wise, to express such ideas and thoughts in a general meeting of the church or fellowship. The body of Christ as a whole still struggles with stereotypical thinking about weight-related issues. And yet, groups of Christians with size issues in common can offer each other sensitive support and friendship, which will help to release us from these stereotypes.

In our current culture, even in church culture, weight is a mark against a woman—unjustly so. However, it is time that Christian women of size stop expecting and accepting treatment as if they were God's lesser children. It is time the thin obsession of the westernized church is recognized as not only prejudice but also part of the sin that God is dealing with in these days of great outpouring of revival fire.

Until that happens, I, for one, no longer consider those people who are thinner than I am automatically to be more spiritual or more valued by God than I am. I fit into the body of Christ because He determined I would. I'm not going away just because I'm viewed as larger than acceptable. No longer will I be a victim of the spiritual snobbery that can come because of size and appearance obsessions within the church.

Have I always thought this way? Sadly, no. Once I was a spiritual, size-prejudiced snob myself. And do you know who was hurt the most by my self-righteousness? I was. And how did I learn this? By the mercy of God, who trusted me enough to take me through some very rough and difficult places with my own weight. Some of us, it seems, learn our best lessons the hard way.

Now I call the church to examine her ways, to look inside her own heart. I call for every Christian to confess his or her sin of inner secret snobbery and self-righteousness in dealing with weight issues and overweight Christians. Then I ask you to join me in asking for God's forgiveness, cleansing, and restoration to the place where He can use us. His love really does come in a size that fits us all perfectly, and glorifies Him as well.

My precious Heavenly Father, we have had enough of self-righteousness and prejudicial attitudes toward ourselves and others. Help us find those safe places within the church where we can drop our guard and find true friends who understand us and our needs as Christian women of size. Bless those who offer us unconditional love. Bless those as well who treat us with contempt because of our size.

Lord, give our pastors revelation and wisdom when they deal with people of size, and show them their hidden hurtful attitudes. Help us love them even when they make hurtful remarks; show us if we are to speak to them or just pray for them. Thank You for showering us with an abundance of unconditional love. Let us live this life within the context of the body of the church to Your glory. In Jesus' name, amen.

Section Six

MOMENT OF DECISION, MOMENT OF TRUTH

Chapter Fifteen

NOTHING LESS THAN A MIRACLE

*N*ow it's time for you to make a decision. I've given you as much of the whole picture as I know. I've put my best effort into writing this book, and you've gone to the personal expense of buying it and investing your time in reading it. I've covered lots of factual territory and emotionally charged material. I have tried to give a clear picture of my position and how I came to embrace it. I have taken on a grave responsibility by writing this book. I am aware that it will be a turning point for many who read it. I am also aware that I could and probably will anger many others.

Some of you will write me letters. Many will be complimentary; many will express anger and hurt. A few will even feel as if I've betrayed them and have simply sought a profitable way to justify my weight regain. I anticipated all of that when I began working on this project. I prayed about it and sensed it was the Lord's direction not only for my life but for my work. In short, I've risked it all—my reputation, my ministry, and my writing career. However, I think it's time we realize that every day we face difficulties that stretch, pull, and strain us, difficulties that test and polish us as we grow to be more like Christ. Some situations are harder than others. Certainly being a large Christian in a thin-obsessed church culture is a tough way to live and love. But even so, God calls us to live at peace with each other.

So what have I actually said in this book? Before we explore the lifestyle choices that face us as women of size, let me summarize what this book has been about.

1. We are not a mistake: neither are we faulty.

For you created my inmost being; you knit me together in my mother's womb. I praise you because I am fearfully and wonderfully made; your works are wonderful, I know that full well. My frame was not hidden from you when I was made in the secret place. When I was woven together in the depths of the earth, your eyes saw my unformed body.

PSALM 139:13-16

Your genetic predisposition, as well as mine, is not a plot against us. If God was truly there even before we were born, and I believe the Bible when it says He was, then God's plan is *for* our lives—not against us. You are a miracle. No matter how big, no matter how many times you've tried to fit into a thin, "ideal"-sized body and failed. You *are* a miracle no matter what size you are at this very moment.

For many who read this book, trying to get thin is like trying to improve on perfection. The world may say you are less than perfect, but God says in Christ you're more than OK!

2. Jesus died to save, not condemn, "whosoever"—even you and me!

For God so loved the world that he gave his one and only Son, that whoever believes in him shall not perish but have eternal life. For God did not send his Son into the world to condemn the world, but to save the world through him. Whoever believes in him is not condemned, but whoever does not believe stands condemned already because he has not believed in the name of God's one and only Son.

JOHN 3:16-18

It is the world that makes us want to measure up in some way before we can be totally accepted. It is secular culture that would make us qualify to fit into its mold before letting us feel valued and worthy. God loves people, sinners and all. He died for our sins, not our size!

3. My body is—and isn't—me.

I think it is right to refresh your memory as long as I live in the tent of this body, because I know that I will soon put it aside.

2 PETER 1:13-14

Peter, the apostle, called his body a tent. He recognized that he wouldn't die when his body died but that in death he would merely put his body "aside." He lived inside his body, just as you and I do. The real me lives inside. I "wear" my body. My body isn't me—not the real inside me.

And I don't live in this body alone. I've invited God to live inside my heart and dwell in my body as well. He accepted me just the way I am and chose to come into my heart upon invitation.

> Do you not know that your body is a temple of the Holy Spirit?
>
> 1 Corinthians 6:19

4. God's love is "one size fits all."

> God has poured out his love into our hearts by the Holy Spirit, whom he has given us. You see, at just the right time, when we were still powerless, Christ died for the ungodly. Very rarely will anyone die for a righteous man, though for a good man someone might possibly dare to die. But God demonstrates his own love for us in this: While we were still sinners, Christ died for us.
>
> Romans 5:5-8

God's love is not targeted only for the average; petite and large-sized persons can receive His love as well. God's love is all encompassing, stretchable, universal, and completely available to all who will accept it. It isn't based on our perfection or self-improvement efforts. Its flow isn't stopped by our failures, nor can it be held back by self- or other-imposed standards of perfection and acceptability. It is given freely, and it never runs out. God loves—end of story.

You can't stop Him from loving me, and you can't make Him stop loving you. No matter how many times you've been excluded because of a physical attribute or your appearance, you can't stop God from including you in the offer of His love-born plan of salvation by faith in His Son, Jesus Christ.

5. God gives us wholesome dignity, not sinful pride.

"For in him we live and move and have our being." As some of your own poets have said, "We are his off-spring."

ACTS 17:28

You may have read material on size acceptance in the past that has turned you off. Material that has at its core a more prideful attitude that has offended your Christian beliefs. If you have heard me say that the size-acceptance position I have come to is a matter of personal pride, you have misunderstood. It is a position of acceptance, of God-given peace—certainly not a position of pride. As children of God, we deserve our full standing as members of the redeemed. As children of God we are to be transformed into His image, not molded into the impossible and unforgiving image of the world (see Rom 12:1-2).

6. The promises of God's Word are not related to weight or size.

For no matter how many promises God has made, they are "Yes" in Christ. And so through him the "Amen" is spoken by us to the glory of God. Now it is God who makes both us and you stand firm in Christ. He anointed us, set his seal of ownership on us, and put his Spirit in our hearts as a deposit, guaranteeing what is to come.

2 CORINTHIANS 1:20-22

When we make weight a prerequisite of receiving any of God's promises, we mishandle the truth of God's Word. The only requirement we have in living the Christian life is to have Christ live in our hearts by faith. Our success as Christians does not depend on us in any way—including our abilities, our appearance, our financial or social status, our race, or our size. Our success as Christians depends on only one thing—God making us stand firm, anointing us with the seal of the Holy Spirit stamped within our hearts.

7. God is more interested in the condition of my heart than in my waist measurement.

You were taught, with regard to your former way of life, to put off your old self, which is being corrupted by its deceitful desires; to be made new in the attitude of your minds; and to put on the new self, created to be like God in true righteousness and holiness.

EPHESIANS 4:22-24

That's what this book is about: a new attitude of our minds. Rejoicing in the fact that we are new creations—not because we've changed our image or lost a ton of weight but because Christ has changed our hearts and lives. We are already new selves, being changed daily with the hope of becoming like God in true righteousness and holiness.

In Christ we have exchanged our old nature for God's nature. No longer do we have to pretend to be jovial or jolly fat people; we are filled with the genuine joy of our salvation. We don't have to wait until we get thin to release the real woman inside us. Through joy and faith in Jesus Christ, she is out!

8. **God graces Christian women of size with gifts just like He does everyone else.**

We have different gifts, according to the grace given us. If a man's gift is prophesying, let him use it in proportion to his faith. If it is serving, let him serve; if it is teaching, let him teach; if it is encouraging, let him encourage; if it is contributing to the needs of others, let him give generously; if it is leadership, let him govern diligently; if it is showing mercy, let him do it cheerfully.

ROMANS 12:6-8

God's gifts are given according to His grace—not according to our weight, weight loss, or pleasing appearance. To give us gifts to use for kingdom purposes based on something as changing as what is socially acceptable or even desirable would make God subject to human whims. God can and will use those who are available to Him, those who are yielded and submissive to His will and His ways. God longs to actively support those whose hearts are completely His, regardless of size or appearance (see 2 Chr 16:9).

The New, True Beloved Me

In other words, we are wanted and loved at any size, in any shape. We are worth redemption no matter what our physical appearance.

My lover spoke and said to me, "Arise, my darling, my beautiful one, and come with me. See! The winter is past;

the rains are over and gone. Flowers appear on the earth; the season of singing has come, the cooing of doves is heard in our land. The fig tree forms its early fruit; the blossoming vines spread their fragrance. Arise, come, my darling; my beautiful one, come with me."

SONG OF SOLOMON 2:10-12

God has wonderful plans for us, my friend. Plans to give us a future and hope (see Jer 29:11) as well as hope for the future (see Jer 31:17). There is no reason to go on hating ourselves or our bodies one moment longer. In fact, we have every reason to respect these bodies of ours no matter what their size, to give them the care we would give them if they were thin.

While the world looks at our bodies with prejudicial eyes, God never does. To Him we are beautiful, because beauty is in the heart of our beloved Beholder. We may be big, but to God we are also beautiful. When Christ lives within us and our lives are found in Him, He cherishes us.

How long has it been since you felt cherished and loved without condition? God's love is offered to you, and the only condition He makes is that you receive Him. Will you do that? Will you put down your size-related excuses and just let God love you? I promise He will not disappoint you!

*M*y precious, beloved Father, I receive Your love anew. I ask you to let me experience Your love at a level I never thought possible before. Thank You for showing me that You don't condemn me. Thank You for sending Your Son, Jesus, to make it possible for me to come to You without reservation, without shame. Help me, Lord, to walk in Your ways, to know Your will concerning my life. I choose to walk in a close love-relationship with You. You are my Beloved, and I am Yours. I thankfully accept Your love banner over me. Amen.

Chapter Sixteen

BIG, BOLD, AND BEAUTIFUL HEALTH AND BEAUTY TIPS

*W*hen the message of this book fully sinks in, you will be changed. I am different, and you can be too. In Christ, you can have peace with your body—yes, you really can. And, once you do, you will never look at life the same way again.

Learn to Live a New Way

Throughout this book, you have not once heard me say that just because you are large, you can throw good discipline and healthy choices out the window. For more than twenty years I have been a major voice for balanced eating and healthy lifestyles. That has not changed. If you will ever make the transforming change to accepting yourself as you are, you must make healthy lifestyle choices to support your decision. Nothing sabotages a large person's sense of worth faster than a food binge!

So how do I do it? How do I maintain my healthy, though larger, outlook and daily life? Let me give you a few big, bold, and beautiful tips for being big, bold, and beautiful.

Appreciate your body as it is.

Consider your body God's temple, not your personal curse. When Jesus Christ paid for our sins with His own life, He did it so that we could live without guilt and shame. His death, not the size of your waist, made your body fit for the indwelling of God's Holy Spirit. The Bible says you are God's temple (see 1 Cor 6:19).

Think twice before risking your body with unhealthy habits or choices.

How can we honor God if we treat the temple *He has chosen* with disrespect? Treat your body with healthy respect and with respect for your health.

Realize that God decided we should all be different.

Take the emphasis off the "package"—your body—and put it on the condition of your heart—both spiritually and physically.

Learn to laugh with a new joy in the Lord.

The daily life of the healthy large person requires strength—inner strength. You won't get inner strength from lifting weights or jogging five miles each morning (though neither is a bad idea). Inner strength comes from the joy of the Lord. And the source of this joy is turning our attention from self to the Savior—praising Him for all He has done and continues to do! As we know from Scripture:

• We are called to enter His gates each and every morning with thanksgiving and His courts with praise (see Ps 100:4).

- Know that He inhabits your praises (see Ps 22:3, KJV), that He comes close to those who praise Him.

- Understand that in the presence of the Lord there is full-ness of joy (see 1 Chr 29:22) and that His joy is your strength (see Neh 8:10).

- Let the joy of the Lord sharpen and refresh your sense of humor. Learn to look at your body as the container of the Lord's joy. Think of yourself as the container of God's joyful Holy Spirit. A cleverly marketed gag gift so popular a few years ago was nothing more than a simple can that gave off peals of laughter when tipped. When you are laughing, think of it as God's way of laughing right out loud. Not at you—*through you*. How else can our lost and troubled world connect with a joyful God except through us?

See your body type and size as a part of your physical heritage.
I love the image described in Psalm 139:13: "For you created my inmost being; you knit me together in my mother's womb." All one has to do is look at an ultrasound image of an unborn child to get a new understanding of the secret place of pregnancy.

Look at family pictures and find the other large people who formed your physical heritage. You are not an accident. You could have had any parents God wanted. But He chose the ones you had. And in the very secret place of your mother's ovaries and your father's genes, He was busy combining characteristics and planning the structure of your physical body. You are not a mistake; neither is the way you are made.

Get to know the "real you" by listing your inner qualities, gifts, and special talents.

None of your inner qualities, gifts, and special talents are size dependent. Read 1 Corinthians 12:4-11 and recognize your giftings as unique, special, and valuable to God's plan for your life. Then turn to Romans 12:6-8 and count each gift and talent that you possess as a treasure to be used for God's glory.

Offer your special giftedness to the whole body of Christ. Don't withhold yourself from us one moment longer on the flimsy excuse that you're fat and fat people have nothing to offer. God's Word says otherwise! Have you given up singing because of "fat lady" jokes? Take it up again. Have you stopped teaching because you think yourself a poor witness? Get ready! God is about to use you again. Give an account of the hope that is within you. Don't you have more to give your church than excuses? Do you have mercy? Can you pray for people? Do it, for heaven's sake!

Give yourself opportunities to cultivate your spiritual gifts. Invest your self, time, and even your money in making your gifts come alive and grow through practice, lessons, or classes. It's biblical to do so.[1]

Stop living in the past or for the future.

Let this be a new day! Leave the future with God, who said in Jeremiah 29:11, "I know the plans I have for you." He's got plans for you just as He has for me. Live in the present; your life is worth something to God and His kingdom *right now*. Just as it is, just the way you look, at the very size you are at this very moment (see Heb 3:7-15). Today is your day. Don't waste another precious moment of your life. You are a treasure to God. Treasure the life He sent His Son to give you.

Choose to have a new attitude toward yourself.

I know it's not easy. All you have to do is volunteer one week in the church nursery to overhear how Mrs. New Mother gave birth less than three weeks ago and is already thinner than she was when she got pregnant. Attend a women's ministries craft boutique to help raise money for missions and you're sure to get the latest scoop on Mrs. So-and-So, who just dropped thirty pounds nearly overnight. Suddenly, you mentally scope out your own body. This book and all its motivational ideas seem shallow as hopelessness sets in once again. But you can get past all that.

Settle it in your heart that you will have a new attitude, that you will be transformed in your mind, as Romans 12:1-2 encourages us. At the very moment you are tempted to relapse into your old way of thinking, take a deep breath, consciously let God love you at that very moment, and go on with your life and worthwhile activities.

Choose to have a new attitude toward food.

Stop being a dieter. Stop criticizing yourself for choosing a new, healthier attitude. Break the diet mentality and give yourself permission to be a normal person who makes normal, healthy food choices.

Give yourself permission to eat when you're hungry and then stop when you feel the first signs of satisfaction. Enjoy a midmorning piece of fruit without weighing it or seeing how many calories it might contain.

Give yourself permission to enjoy God's plentiful blessings without overdoing it. Choose an attitude of healthy responsibility when portioning out your food at the table. Bless yourself by eating in moderation with thanksgiving to God.

Give yourself a chance to try a simpler approach to meal and menu planning. Learn to think in terms of food preparation rather than focusing on recipes and see how much simpler and healthier your menu becomes.

Acquaint yourself with the different kinds of fats and how they impact your health and heart. Responsibly reconsider sugars and artificial sweeteners. Make your decisions and food choices based on reliable information and personal responsibility, not guilt.

Learn the joy of eating in obedience to the Holy Spirit's inner nudging when you're not sure if you "should or shouldn't" at a buffet table.

Give your body a new chance to move.
There are lots of ways to build a healthy level of activity into your routine without subjecting yourself to the humiliation of appearing in public in spandex. Here are a couple of suggestions for easing yourself into a more active lifestyle.

- Take up walking—fifteen minutes a day to start. Seven minutes out and seven back. Why not give yourself a small tape player or portable CD player for your next birthday or Christmas? Put on some lively praise and worship music and bless the Lord with your heart as you bless your body with healthy physical activity.

- Purchase an exercise videotape especially produced for large women. *Fit for a King* is a Christian video I made with Stormie Omartian just for Christian women of size. Every woman on the tape is large—let its verbal and musical message encourage you to a life of being fit for our King.

Give your new self a new look!

Large women don't have to be "plain Janes." Learn to make the most of your best features—your sparkling eyes, your lovely hands, your beautiful hair. A little extra attention to your appearance first thing in the morning will make a difference in your confidence level for the rest of the day! Try these tips to give yourself—and your appearance—a boost.

- Have your colors done. Why wait until that never-will-come someday when you get thin to see what colors flatter your beautiful complexion?

- Be bold in your accessories. Use the strongest colors you look good in to announce your presence. Assume people like the way you look. Not every glance you receive is an unappreciative one. Attitudes are changing toward larger people. Accept that and get the emotional benefit from it.

- Ask your hairstylist for a new "do." Experiment with a new cut or color. The goal is to be the beautifully confident new you.

- Give yourself a facial and experiment with new makeup. Find your best facial features and enhance them. Go to a department store and get the free makeover. (But don't feel pushed into buying the makeup if you can't afford it.) Look in magazines like *Radiance* or *BBW* for makeup tips and encouragement to be more beautiful than you ever thought you could. When you get catalogs in the mail for large-sized clothing and panty hose, observe how the larger models sit and stand. Examine their hairstyles and makeup.

- Get a new, stylish outfit whenever your budget will allow. Many large women buy cheaper clothes than their thin counterparts simply because they believe that someday soon they may be thin and the money spent on larger sizes will have been wasted. Others, even though it's not true, feel as though they don't deserve anything very nice simply because they are large.

- Match your panty hose to your outfits. You'll be surprised how feminine you feel when you tastefully accent your outfit with black or light ivory panty hose. I love to wear fancy, patterned knee-high pant stockings with slacks. Just a peek of checks, hearts, or tiny dots at my ankles expresses the fanciful feelings I kept tightly contained for far too long.

- Buy the nicest lingerie you can afford. Lots of lace underneath makes me feel like a real woman even when my outer outfit is quite tailored. Buy bras that fit, panties in pastels or bright colors, and indulge in slips that feel luxurious and soft. Don't neglect your nightwear either. Express your feminine side in your loungewear.

- Pay close attention to personal hygiene. Nobody likes offensive body odor. There's no good reason why large people can't smell good and be as clean as anyone else. Find an affordable fragrance that smells good on you. Not all fragrances go well with every person. Mine comes from the local drugstore or supermarket. It's perfect with my body chemistry, and I indulge—even on the days I stay home.

- Have more courage to be yourself. Show your corner of the world that big can be and is beautiful—and you are the living proof!

Renew the realization that this is the only body you will ever have.

You don't just endure a large body for a short while then get to trade it in for a new, different body—not until we get to heaven anyway. But in the meantime, this is it—for life.

Give your body a rest and yourself a break by learning to live in peace with its size. Stop berating your body; stop abusing it with unhealthy food and risky dieting practices. Bless it with physical activity and cherish it with wholesome habits. Serve God in and with your body.

Make a new commitment to a healthy lifestyle—to look better, to feel better, in both body and soul. Make long-range health goals and select food choices that enhance and promote those goals.

Drink more water.

Make it a habit you will never have to break. Take a sipper bottle with you whenever you travel or go to work. Find some way to remind yourself to drink water. Drinking water is essential to good health. It flushes out toxins and waste and does wonders for a woman's skin. Water also helps keep a runaway appetite under control.

Get new role models.

Look for Christian sisters of size who are positive and upbeat about their relationship with Christ and who are involved in His work. There are beautiful big women who have made significant contributions to the kingdom of God. Look at their accomplishments. In writing about large, successful black women for *Ebony* magazine, writer Lisa Jones Townsel said,

> These women have learned to work with every bit God has given them. And although they aren't advocating excessive eating or saying that it's okay to ignore health risks associated with obesity, they do pose one vital question to their critics, as one big-boned beauty has said, "If we are healthy, vibrant and beautiful, why change?"[2]

What positive role models for us to admire! I have my own personal favorites, but you can make your own list. Just look around.

It's a New Day

You and I have struggled far too long. It's time we found a new way to measure our success as people and our worth as Christians, apart from the numbers on the bathroom scale. It's time we stopped obsessing and thinking of food as evil and tormenting ourselves because we still can't fit into a size 9.

So I challenge you. Get off the scale and bury other habits that reinforce a destructive dieting mentality. Quit thinking of yourself as "good" when you stay within some arbitrarily set calorie limit and "bad" when you think you have "blown it." Feeling disgusted with yourself does not contribute to your new healthy, moderate lifestyle. Instead ask God to help you learn when you are hungry. Ask Him to heal the systems in your body so that you know when you've had enough to eat. Depend on the Lord to help you choose a whole new approach to food that provides you with some flexibility for your busy life and schedule.

You are a marvelous person, and your body is a miraculous machine. When it comes to self-control and health issues, you are the one bearing the responsibility, and you must make the final choices. Why not learn to live big, bold, and beautiful through giving your body the best care possible? God will help you—just ask Him.

My Heavenly Father, I choose to accept my larger body and the responsibility for taking care of it. I choose this day to make, in the best possible way, a big, bold, and beautiful new beginning as I seek ways to express the joy and beauty You have given me. Show me the beauty You see in me. Help me see the beauty You have placed in all Your redeemed larger women. Help me make wise choices in the food I eat and in the exercise I do.

I bless You for the gifts You have given me, and I choose to let them be stirred within me once again. Thank You for being so patient with me until I came to this place in my life. Help me to be patient and forgiving toward myself for the things I have done in my body, trying to get thin, and for the time I've wasted being unloving and unforgiving toward myself for being fat. Give me the strength I'll need to live wholly for You and Your glory—now, in this new day, this new way, just the way I am. In Jesus' name, amen.

Chapter Seventeen

FREE TO BE ME—
AND ALL GOD WANTS ME TO BE!

*Y*es, it's true, by the time I was in my midtwenties, I was on a mission. Misguided, to be sure, but wholly committed to my goal. I was what you could accurately term *determined*. So very sure that thin was out there waiting for me, with every ounce of my plump self I was bound to get it. And I wasn't much different from other women I knew. I hated the agony of being fat, and with all that was in me, I determined to end that agony once and for all.

Each succeeding failure brought me so much emotional pain that you'd think I would have learned my lesson. But the sad truth is, being on the mission had replaced being me. I was absolutely nothing if not committed to my mission. In spite of a calamitously long list of failed attempts at being thin, I believed that the right diet, program, or pill would someday miraculously appear.

In the process, I did learn to control food binges. I did learn to eat in obedience to body signals and bring my behaviors and habits under the control of the Holy Spirit. The fruit of the Spirit was evident in my life at all levels. I brought order into my housekeeping, I learned to make good use of my time, and I discovered my spiritual gifts and God-given talents for writing and speaking.

But I could not find a permanent way to stay thin. Tragically, I was on the verge of believing myself a complete failure.

Somehow, God's still, small voice managed to penetrate my daily quiet times. His reassurance of love and acceptance came, quietly at first, then louder and clearer as I began to reach toward Him receptively.

Finally, the life of go-nowhere dieting came to an end. Self-hatred and resentment for my body slowly gave way as freedom began to seep into the edges of my very soul. Then I took another turn and wondered, without the passionate anguish of my mission, if I even knew who I was. Did I even have an identity apart from a large-trying-to-get-thin person? Was the life I put on the back burner while I pursued my goal weight still available?

When I was totally focused on the illusive, obsessive dream of being thin, my life, though not my body, was literally shaped around my quest. Everything I did was centered around my goal—my shopping, my wishing, my dreaming, my creativity, my work, my hopes, and even my faith—all had a *someday* kind of quality. It became imperative to my survival to virtually ignore all my other problems while using all my energy trying to control only one thing—my weight. I'm sure I don't have to tell you that one day I found a neglected, undernourished person inside.

But as you know by now, all that has changed. In Christ, I have discovered the freedom of living a normal life. I no longer pin all my expectations and hopes on being thin. I focus my attention on letting the Holy Spirit work within me, changing my heart, hoping someday to more perfectly reflect Christ's image. I no longer let my successes, gifts, and accomplishments be eclipsed by the bathroom scale.

It was more than a bit painful, to say the least, putting aside the preoccupation with self-improvement and choosing spiritual growth instead. Weak, battered, and beaten, I looked to God for relief. Thankfully, miraculously, I found it in His perfect, nonjudgmental love and care.

But the challenge was absolutely overwhelming. For most people, this decision has ramifications in the family, a few friends, and perhaps church. But for me, the risk included my public, ministerial identity. All I knew that made me feel secure and valuable to God's work and kingdom was left hanging in the balance. Needless to say, for a time, at least in the beginning, there was a lot of lying around on the couch crying.

However, I began to sense something a lot more satisfactory, substantial, and rewarding than the superficial victories of the past, such as making it through a wedding without even a morsel of cake. I sensed a new level of inner victory as I became acquainted with my real self, perhaps for the first time. You see, when the total pursuit of our life's work hinges on being able to get and maintain "thin," many of us become someone we don't even know. Without even fully realizing it—and while the public, successful *thin* writer, author, and speaker Neva Coyle was having to fade away—the real, inner-person Neva Coyle was struggling to come to life. Both experiences brought me moments of sheer horror. My family had to adjust to having me around the house more just as they had to adjust to the new, bigger me.

"Honey," I said one night as my husband and I enjoyed the hot tub in our backyard. "Am I too fat for you?"

"No," he replied. "You're too fat for you. I accept you at

any size. You have to learn to do the same." I don't know what I would have done had he complained about my weight regain. If there had even been a hint of a lack of support I would have given up rather than chosen to go on.

Soon afterward, the most incredible of all discoveries suddenly emerged. When I put aside the superhuman, superspiritual efforts to become a woman of value (a status I had assumed would be found only with thinness, of course) I discovered that *I already was!*

It's hard for many people to think that a weight and appearance issue could hold so much power over an otherwise intelligent woman. But I'm certainly not the only American woman who has lost her ability to live and even laugh spontaneously because of her battle with weight and its tyranny. Afraid that my tummy might shake unattractively, I had taught myself to neither laugh nor cry in front of anyone—friends and strangers alike. But when I discovered that God loved me on a grander scale, I relaxed. After all, I am loved by the eternal, almighty God who made me—tummy and all.

Of course, I braced myself for thoughtless comments. I was sure that being free wouldn't exclude me from the rudeness that seems perfectly acceptable if the target is someone who's thought less than perfect. But I'm still waiting, and it simply hasn't happened. I have come to the conclusion that when I accept myself, others are more free to accept me as well.

Large people are not usually the ones who grace the covers of national magazines or serve as spokespersons on TV commercials, but I refuse to let that rob me of my personal validation as a Christian or as a larger woman. It isn't a connection with my culture that makes me feel worthwhile and loved; it is a connection to God through

His Son, Jesus Christ. For too long I believed that being thin was the missing link to happiness, but I was wrong. That's not biblical truth at all. In Christ I am free—free to be worthwhile, free to be happy—free to be me.

This new freedom has brought me face to face with the trash I had accepted as essential truth. For example, there was the thought that I was only wanted when I was thin—or at least trying to get that way. I also thought that no one would love me just the way I was and that people wouldn't want to hug my larger, softer body. I thought I wouldn't be pretty anymore.

Then I replaced that trash with *treasure.*

Now I accept that I am a wanted person. Jesus died for me so that I could be in relationship with the Father—*because He wants me.* Many people love me. Just like this, just the way I am. I am one of the most hugged women I know. Women and men, children and even teenagers hug me each and every week at my church. If I see them in the market, they hug me. When I go to one of the restaurants here in my hometown I am hugged by the owner. I am hugged when I speak at a retreat and when I happen upon a friend I haven't seen for a long time. And I'm hugged at home.

And pretty? I still love complimentary colors, nice clothes, and doing my hair in its usual soft style. I shop for attractive frames when I get glasses, and carefully do my makeup each morning before I leave for the office (where I usually see no one all day!). But my beauty routine doesn't stop there. Using 1 Peter 3:3-5 as my beauty guide ...

Your beauty should not come from outward adornment, such as braided hair and the wearing of gold jewelry and fine clothes. Instead, it should be that of your inner self, the unfading beauty of a gentle and quiet spirit, which is of great worth in God's sight. For this is the way the holy women of the past who put their hope in God used to make themselves beautiful.

... I fill my mind and heart with praises to God through worship tapes and a regular daily devotional habit. I write upbeat insights I get from Scripture in my journal and maintain an active prayer life. I'm finished with second-guessing and wasting precious time.

Romans 12:2 says, "Be transformed by the renewing of your mind." Yes, my friend, I'm living proof: I may not be thin, but I am certainly transformed!

I'm a very thankful woman. Thankful to my friends for their support in the long, miserable days, weeks, and months during my weight regain and the depression that went with it. Thankful to the readers who kept reading my books and writing wonderful letters of encouragement as they followed my progress. Also, I'm thankful for my church, for the pastors who have counseled me through the years and encouraged me to stay in ministry when I felt disqualified and unworthy. I'm thankful for prayer partners who pray for me every day. And I'm thankful for my family members, who love me just for being me—whatever my size.

And, as strange as it sounds, I'm also thankful to me. For learning to look in the mirror and smile. For having the courage to walk in this new, untried freedom. For not giving up on myself and caving into the pressure to try yet another life-risking weight-loss plan.

But most of all, I'm thankful to God for His tremendous love and care. Thankful to Him for His patience and gentle

long-suffering with me as I have come to love and understand His Word more than ever before. Thankful for the
freedom to be me—and all He wants me to be. I'm grateful
to Him for the opportunity to write this book and for leading me to the right editors, Gwen Ellis and Heidi Hess, and
to the wonderful publishing staff at Servant Publications.

And I'm thankful for you. Thankful that you have taken
the time and made the sacrifice to read this book. I look for-
ward to hearing how God used the words on these pages to
help you recognize and realize how much He loves you on a
much grander scale than you could ever imagine. Here is the
prayer I am praying for you today:

*D*ear Father, the person holding this book
needs You to love her the way You have loved me.
Without reservation, without judgment. The hands
holding these pages need to grasp hold of Your
hands in a new, tighter, securer grip as this woman
finds the courage to be who You say she is, who You
made her to be.

Bless the eyes that read these words, dear God,
that they may help this person see You in a new way.
That she may come to see herself differently because
of who You say she is.

Bless the mind that processes these sentences into
complete thoughts and the heart that receives this
message. Transform the person reading this prayer
into the beautiful person You have destined her to
become.

Thank You for loving us, Father—loving us on a
grander scale. Amen.

Notes

INTRODUCTION

1. Deborah Gregory, "Heavy judgment: a sister talks about the pain of living large," *Essence*, August 1994, 57.

ONE
Where Does It All Begin?

1. "Painted Babies," a program broadcast on The Learning Channel, December 21, 1996.
2. Eva Pomice, "I'm So Fat! When kids hate their bodies," *Redbook*, April 1995, 184.
3. Mary Phipher, Ph.D., *Reviving Ophelia* (New York: Grosset/Putnam, 1994), 68.
4. Phipher, 55.

TWO
Being Thin for Him

1. Judith Rodin, "Body Mania," *Psychology Today*, January-February 1992, 56.
2. Rosemary Bray, "Heavy Burden: Women who are pressured by society to be beautiful," *Essence*, January 1992, 52.
3. Rodin, 56.
4. David M. Garner and Ann Kearny-Cooke, "Body Image, 1996: There may be a shift in how people view themselves," *Psychology Today*, March–April 1996, 55.
5. Rodin, 56.
6. Rodin, 56.
7. Jordan Paul, Ph.D., and Margaret Paul, Ph.D., *Do I Have to Give Up Me to Be Loved by You?* (Minneapolis: CompCare, 1993), 177.
8. Paul and Paul, 169.

THREE
At What Price Beauty?

1. Richard Corliss, "Dream Girls," *Time,* September 18, 1995, 102.
2. Scott Brown, "Pursuit of Perfection," *Time* (special issue on California), November 18, 1991, 88.
3. Based on information from "No real-life Barbies and Kens: Studies show that average American men and women fall far short of the physical ideals represented by Ken and Barbie dolls," *Industry Week,* May 6, 1996, 15.
4. As quoted by Annemarie Iverson in "A world without beauty rules," *Harper's Bazaar,* October 1993, 258.
5. Ellen Welty, "Could they really make me look younger?" *Redbook,* December 1995, 70.
6. Bonnie Davidson, "Coping with the worst part of your body," *Cosmopolitan,* November 1990, 298.

FOUR
Beautiful Is Not the Same as Lovable

1. Esther D. Rothboum, "Does Overweight Hold You Back?" *Weight Watchers Magazine,* May 1996, 46.
2. Laura Muha, "Don't Call Us...We'll Call You," *Weight Watchers Magazine,* November 1995, 40.
3. Daniel Seligman, "Fat Chances," *Fortune,* May 20, 1991, 155. See also Martin Everett, "Fat Chance: Let an overweight person call on your best customers?" *Sales & Marketing Management,* March 1990, 66.
4. Leslie Lampert, "Fat Like Me," *Ladies Home Journal,* May 1993, 154.
5. Gregory, 57.
6. Leslie Lampert, "Can a Woman Be Fat and Happy?" *Ladies Home Journal,* March 1995, 120.
7. D.M. Garner and S.C. Wolley, "Confronting the failure of behavioral and dietary treatments for obesity," *Clinical Psychology Review* 11 (1991): 729–80.
8. Lampert, "Can a Woman Be Fat and Happy?" 120.

FIVE
Dieting: The Sure Way to Defeat

1. Joel Gurin, "Leaner, not lighter: why you need to rethink your beliefs about dieting before you start," *Psychology Today,* June 1989, 32.
2. Anne Broccolo-Philbin, "An obsession with being painfully thin," *Current Health,* January 1996, 23.
3. Broccolo-Philbin, 23.
4. Deborah Wilson, "Starved for love?" *Chatelaine,* February 1997, 49.

TWELVE
I'm Big—Not Sick!

1. Jaclyn Packer, Ph.D., "Dr. Fat Attack," *Psychology Today,* March-April 1994, 10.
2. W. Charisse Goodman, *The Invisible Woman* (Carlsbad, Calif.: Gurze Books, 1995), 20.
3. Shelley Bovey, *The Forbidden Body* (London: Pandora/ HarperCollins, 1994), 45.
4. Bovey, 45.
5. Bovey, 45.
6. Bovey, 45.
7. Dr. William Bennett, speaking at the National Association to Advance Fat Awareness Convention in Columbus, Ohio, 1982, quoted in *Size Acceptance and Self Acceptance—the NAAFA Workbook,* 1.
8. Lynn Meletche, quoted in *Size Acceptance & Self Acceptance,* 36.
9. Garner and Wolley, 729–80.
10. *The Healthy Weight Journal,* 402 South Fourteenth Street, Hettinger, North Dakota 58639.

THIRTEEN
Surviving the Minefields of the Fat War

1. Goodman, 9.
2. *The Healthy Weight Journal,* January–February 1997, 7.

3. Stephen Barrett, M.D., "Quackery by Mail," QuackWatch web site, http://www.quackwatch.com.

4. David Stipp, "New Weapons in the War on Fat," *Fortune*, February 5, 1996.

5. "The New Miracle Drug?" *Time*, September 23, 1996.

6. Robert's remarks can be found on the Internet: http://web.mit.edu/dumit/www/wld2-rm-4.html.

7. Robert Langreth and Laura Johannes, "Redux maker underplays risks, doctors say," *Wall Street Journal*, 1996, quoted in the Internet web site, http://www.kentuckycon...ws/1124/ffront4re.html.

8. Langreth and Johannes, "Redux."

9. Lynn McAfee, director, Medical Project, Council on Weight and Size Discrimination, e-mail to author, September 27, 1996.

10. Bruce Bower, "Gene pain may incite obesity, depression," *Science News*, September 21, 1996, 181.

11. Charles D. Bankhead, "Vices, vanities: hot topics for clinical pharmacologists," *Medical World News*, April 25, 1988, 36.

12. Frank Murray, "Hydroxycitric acid: The weight is over," *Better Nutrition for Today's Living*, November 1994, 34.

13. Advice and tips are based on remarks from QuackWatch Home Page at http://www.quackwatch.com.

FOURTEEN
Church Life and the Christian Woman of Size

1. Reuben Welch, *We Really Do Need Each Other* (Grand Rapids, Mich.: Zondervan, 1975), 27.

2. Michael Slater, *Stretcher Bearers* (Ventura, Calif.: Regal, 1985).

SIXTEEN
Big, Bold, and Beautiful Health and Beauty Tips

1. See Matthew 25:20; 1 Timothy 4:7; and 2 Timothy 1:6.

2. Lisa Jones Townsel, "Big Is Beautiful," *Ebony*, February 1997, 162.

To write to Neva Coyle, or for information
on having her speak in your area or church, write to:

Neva Coyle
P.O. Box 1638
Oakhurst, CA 93644

NCoyle@compuserve.com

ANOTHER BOOK FROM
Neva Coyle

A Woman of Strength
Reclaim Your Past, Seize Your Present, and Secure Your Future

What's the difference between a strong woman and a woman of strength? Why does one send everyone scurrying toward the nearest exit, while the other draws people to her? Can a woman learn to be more capable, more victorious, and more decisive without being overbearing?

In *A Woman of Strength,* Neva Coyle helps readers to reclaim their past, redeem their pain, and redirect their focus to meet the challenges of life with grace and courage. Through stories of women who discovered their own strength, the author shows us that the present is an opportunity to heal from the past, and that the future can be exciting territory to explore with confidence. *220 pages, $10.99*